Unsung Warriors

Azadi Ka Amrit Mahotsav is an initiative of the Government of India to commemorate and celebrate 75 years of Independence and the glorious history of its people, culture and achievements.

The festival is dedicated to the people of India, who are not only instrumental in leading India in its evolutionary journey, but also have within them the power and potential to enable Prime Minister Narendra Modi's vision of activating India 2.0. A Self-reliant India.

The official journey of Azadi Ka Amrit Mahotsav began on 12 March, 2021, starting a 75-week countdown to the 75th anniversary of our independence, and will end on 15 August, 2023.

Unsung Warriors

Aditi Sharma

Published by
PRABHAT PRAKASHAN PVT. LTD.
4/19 Asaf Ali Road,
New Delhi-110 002 (INDIA)
e-mail: prabhatbooks@gmail.com

ISBN 978-93-5521-768-4
UNSUNG WARRIORS
by Ms. Aditi Sharma

Edition
First, 2023

Paperback Price
₹ 350.00 (Rupees Three Hundred Fifty only)

Printed at
R-Tech Offset Printers, Delhi

Jagat Prakash Nadda
National President

Bharatiya Janata Party

Date : 26 March, 2022

Message

Millions of Indians made innumerable sacrifices to liberate the country from the clutches of foreign rulers. However, only very few of them could get recognition in the eyes of public and majority of them could not find due place in the history of Independent India. Therefore, an effort has been made to bring in fore the sacrifices made by those forgotten and unsung heroes of our freedom struggle.

Hon'ble PM Sh. Narendra Modiji has envisaged the Vision of Amrit Mahotsav, on completion of 75 years of India's Independence. I am happy to know that on this occasion which is also the beginning of Amrit Kaal, a book is being compiled encompassing the contributions of all those forgotten heroes and freedom fighters.

I take this opportunity to complement and extend my best wishes to the successful compilation of the book 'Unsung Warriors' by Ms. Aditi Sharma.

(Jagat Prakash Nadda)

6-A, Deendayal Upadhyay Marg, New Delhi-110 002 Phone: 011-23500000

अमित शाह

गृह मंत्री एवं सहकारिता मंत्री
भारत सरकार

संदेश

यह अत्यंत हर्ष का विषय है कि भारतीय जनता युवा मोर्चा, दिल्ली द्वारा 'UNSUNG WARRIORS' नामक पुस्तक का प्रकाशन किया जा रहा है।

यह वर्ष हम आजादी के अमृत महोत्सव वर्ष के रूप में मना रहे हैं। यह आजादी लाखों लोगों के त्याग और बलिदान के कारण संभव हो पाई। स्वतंत्र भारत का हर एक व्यक्ति आज इन वीरों और महापुरुषों का ऋणी है, जिन्होंने अपना संपूर्ण जीवन देश की आजादी के लिए समर्पित कर दिया। प्रधानमंत्री श्री नरेंद्र मोदीजी के नेतृत्व में हमने यह तय किया है कि आजादी के आंदोलन के सभी शहीदों की अमर गाथा को जन-जन तक पहुँचाएँगे। आपके द्वारा संगृहीत इन महान् पुरुषों की जीवन-गाथा पर आधारित पुस्तक हम सभी को स्वतंत्रता संग्राम की याद दिलाती रहेगी और देश-प्रेम की भावना के प्रति प्रेरणा देती रहेगी।

इसी दिशा में आपका यह प्रयास सराहनीय है। मैं 'UNSUNG WARRIORS' पुस्तक के सफल प्रकाशन हेतु अपनी शुभकानाएँ प्रेषित करता हूँ।

(अमित शाह)

कार्यालय : गृह मंत्रालय, नॉर्थ ब्लाक, नई दिल्ली-110001 • दूरभाष : 23092462, 23094686
फैक्स : 23094221 • इ-मेल : hm@nic.in

धर्मेंद्र प्रधान
ଧର୍ମେନ୍ଦ୍ର ପ୍ରଧାନ
Dharmendra Pradhan

सत्यमेव जयते

मंत्री
शिक्षा; कौशल विकास
और उद्यमशीलता, भारत सरकार
Minister
Education; Skill Development &
Entrepreneurship
Government of India

Message

I am pleased to learn that team of Bharatiya Janata Yuva Morcha, a book 'UNSUNG WARRIORS' to re-memorise and express gratitude towards unsung and unknown freedom fighters who fought for India's freedom.

In today's fast-moving and competitive day-to-day life, it is not easy to find time to explore our rich heritage and glorious past. This becomes even crucial whilst the nation celebrates Azadi ka Amrit Mahotsav (commemoration of 75 years of Indian Independence).

As I understand, this book attempts to recall and remember forgotten heroes of our freedom struggle, many of whom might be renowned yet unknown to the new generation. The aim of recreating and bringing forth stories, which lay as faded memories of the past, shall serve as a medium of inspiration and encouragement for the coming generations. The spirit of India is incomplete whilst we take our unsung heroes along this journey of growth and development. Their ethos and principles. ought to be recalled and respected.

I am sure this book acknowledges the unsung heroes of Indian Independence who have struggled and sacrificed their life for nationalism and congratulate the compiles and the publisher for their praiseworthy efforts. Undoubtedly it is going to motivate, inspire and encourage the masses.

(Dharmendra Pradhan)

New Delhi
30th May, 2022

सबको शिक्षा, अच्छी शिक्षा

कौशल भारत, कुशल भारत

MOE - Room No. 3, 'C' Wing, 3rd Floor, Shastri Bhavan, New Delhi-110 115, Phone: 91-11-23782387, Fax: 91-11-23382365 MSDE - Room No. 516, 5th Floor, Shram Shakti Bhawan, Rafi Marg, New Delhi-110001, Phone: 91-11-23465810, Fax: 011-23465825 E-mail: minister.sm@gov.in, minister-msde@gov.in

अनुराग सिंह ठाकुर
ANURAG SINGH THAKUR

सत्यमेव जयते

मंत्री
सूचना एवं प्रसारण और
युवा कार्यक्रम व खेल, भारत सरकार
Minister
Information & Broadcasting
and Youth Affairs & Sports
Government of India

संदेश

मुझे यह जानकर प्रसन्नता हुई है कि भारतीय जनता युवा मोर्चा, दिल्ली द्वारा 'UNSUNG WARRIORS' नामक पुस्तक का प्रकाशन किया जा रहा है।

इस वर्ष आदरणीय प्रधानमंत्री श्री नरेंद्र मोदीजी के नेतृत्व में हम भारत की स्वतंत्रता के 75वें वर्ष का जश्न 'आजादी का अमृत महोत्सव' के रूप में मना रहे हैं। हम ऐसे गुमनाम नायकों को खोजने में लगे हुए हैं, जिन्होंने स्वतंत्रता संग्राम के दौरान महत्त्वपूर्ण भूमिका निभाई थी, लेकिन एक योजनाबद्ध तरीके से उनके योगदान को हमेशा हाशिए पर रखा गया। उन्हें जो पहचान, जो सम्मान मिलना चाहिए था, जिसके वे हकदार थे, वह उन्हें नहीं दिया गया। ऐसे कई स्वतंत्रता सेनानियों के नाम कई युवाओं को पता नहीं हैं, जिन्होंने स्वतंत्रता संग्राम में अपना योगदान दिया। आजादी के इस 75वें वर्ष का जश्न मनाने के लिए गुमनाम नायकों के योगदान को उजागर करना हम सभी के लिए बहुत सम्मान की बात है। आपके द्वारा संगृहीत इन महान् पुरुषों की जीवन-गाथा पर आधारित पुस्तक हम सभी को स्वतंत्रता संग्राम की याद दिलाती रहेगी और देश-प्रेम की भावना के प्रति प्रेरणा देती रहेगी। निश्चित रूप से इस दिशा में आपके द्वारा किया गया प्रयास अत्यंत सराहनीय है।

मैं 'UNSUNG WARRIORS' पुस्तक के सफल प्रकाशन के लिए अपनी हार्दिक शुभकामनाएँ प्रेषित करता हूँ।

(अनुराग सिंह ठाकुर)

22, अकबर रोड, नई दिल्ली 110001
दूरभाष : +91-11-23012365 • इ-मेल : mphamirpur@gmail.com
22, Akbar Road, New Delhi-110001
Tel. : +91-11-23012365 • E-mail : mphamirpur@gmail.com

ॐ

प्रिय बहन अदिति शर्माजी,

नमस्कार।

यह जानकर अत्यंत हर्ष हुआ कि आपने स्वाधीनता के अमृत महोत्सव के वर्ष में भारत के लंबे संघर्षकाल में लगे अपने वीरों व वीरांगनाओं के प्रति कृतज्ञता प्रकट करने तथा उन्हें श्रद्धांजलि अर्पित करने के लिए महासागर को गागर में भरने का महत्त्वपूर्ण कार्य इस संकलन के रूप में पूर्ण किया है, इसके लिए आप सभी को हार्दिक साधुवाद व शुभकामनाएँ।

जो समाज अपने अतीत को तथा अपने पूर्वजों को भूल जाता है, उसका भविष्य भी अंधकारमय हो जाता है। आपका यह प्रयास इस दिशा में प्रकाश फैलाने का कार्य है। भारत का स्वाधीनता के लिए किया गया संग्राम भारतीय इतिहास का स्वर्ण युग ही है, जिसमें भारत के 'एक जन-एक राष्ट्र' का साक्षात् दर्शन हुआ।

इस संघर्ष में भारत की इंच-इंच भूमि पर स्वधर्म, स्वदेश तथा स्वराज की रक्षा और उसकी प्राप्ति के लिए नगर, ग्राम, वन व गिरिकंदराएँ जाग उठीं, वहाँ रहने वालों में आबालवृद्ध, स्त्री-पुरुष, वर्ग-वर्ण-जाति-संप्रदाय की सीमाएँ लाँघकर तथा सामाजिक, राजनीतिक, धार्मिक तथा शैक्षणिक मनोभाव से ऊपर उठकर भारतमाता की मुक्ति हेतु एक मन हो गए।

इस स्वाधीनता संग्राम की यात्रा में कवि, लेखक, कलाकार, शिक्षक, शिक्षार्थी, वैज्ञानिक, पत्रकार, व्यवसायी, मजदूर, किसान, संत, महात्मा, संन्यासी, साधकों तथा समाज के अन्य सभी विद्वज्जनों ने प्रत्यक्ष या परोक्ष रूप में भारत में रहते हुए और तत्कालीन भारत की सीमाओं के बाहर सुदूर विदेश में भी अपनी-अपनी समझ व सामर्थ्य के अनुसार माँ भारती को अपना अर्घ्य निवेदन किया है। वे आज ज्ञात और अज्ञात हैं, किंतु उनके पावन त्याग व समर्पण से माँ भारती विदेशी जंजीरों से मुक्त हो पाईं, उनका चरित्र हमारे लिए सूर्य के तेजस्वी आलोक के समान है। उस दिशा में किया गया संकलन का यह प्रयास सराहनीय है। इसके लिए आप सभी को पुनः बधाई और स्वराज्य के अमृत महोत्सव की शुभकामनाएँ।

कालजयी माँ भारती के सपूतों को कोटिशः नमन!

जय भारत!

शभेच्छु

अकुमार

(अजय कुमार)

क्षेत्रीय बौद्धिक प्रमुख, उत्तर भारत क्षेत्र, रा.स्व. संघ

सिद्धार्थन
प्रदेश महामंत्री (संगठन)

भारतीय जनता पार्टी, दिल्ली प्रदेश
Bharatiya Janata Party, Delhi Pradesh

शुभ संदेश

मुझे जानकर हर्ष हुआ है कि भारतीय जनता युवा मोर्चा, दिल्ली द्वारा 'UNSUNG WARRIORS' नामक पुस्तक का प्रकाशन किया जा रहा है।

इस वर्ष आदरणीय प्रधानमंत्री श्री नरेंद्र मोदीजी के नेतृत्व में हम भारत की स्वतंत्रता के 75वें वर्ष का जश्न 'आजादी का अमृत महोत्सव' के रूप में मना रहे हैं। हम ऐसे गुमनाम नायकों को खोजने में लगे हुए हैं, जिन्होंने स्वतंत्रता संग्राम के दौरान महत्त्वपूर्ण भूमिका निभाई थी, लेकिन किसी कारण वश उनको उनका सही सम्मान और पहचान नहीं मिल सकी, जिसके वे हकदार थे।

ऐसे कई स्वतंत्रता सेनानियों के नाम कई युवांओं को पता नहीं हैं, जिन्होंने स्वतंत्रता संग्राम में अपना योगदान दिया और कहीं खो गए। इस आजादी के 75वें वर्ष का जश्न मनाने के लिए गुमनाम नायकों के योगदान को उजागर करना हम सभी के लिए बहुत सम्मान की बात है। आपके द्वारा संगृहीत इन महान् पुरुषों की जीवन-गाथा पर आधारित पुस्तक हम सभी को स्वतंत्रता संग्राम की याद दिलाती रहेगी और देश-प्रेम की भावना के प्रति प्रेरणा देती रहेगी। निश्चित रूप से इस दिशा में भारतीय युवा मोर्चा के सभी कार्यकर्ताओं के द्वारा किया गया प्रयास अत्यंत सराहनीय है।

मैं 'UNSUNG WARRIORS' पुस्तक के सफल प्रकाशन के लिए आपनी हार्दिक शुभकामनाएँ प्रेषित करता हूँ।

(सिद्धार्थन)
प्रदेश महामंत्री (संगठन)

14, पंडित पंत मार्ग, नई दिल्ली-110001, दूरभाष / फैक्स : 23712323, 23712744, 23712509
14, Pandit Pant Marg, New Delhi- 110001, Tel / Fax : 23712323, 23712744, 23712509 Mo.: 9213099609, Whatsapp : 9560054357
E-mail : Bjpsidh007@gmail.com

ತೇಜಸ್ವಿ ಸೂರ್ಯ
तेजस्वी सूर्य
TEJASVI SURYA
Member of Parliament (Lok Sabha)
Bengaluru South-Karnataka

MEMBER:
Standing Committee on
Information Technology
Joint Committee on Offices of Profit
Joint Parliamentary Committee
on Personal Data
Protection Bill 2019

Message

New India under Prime Minister Shri Narendra Modiji has witnessed tremendous growth over the last few years in various fields growing from strength to strength. PM Modiji's vision of Atmanirbhar Bharat, encompassing India's larger role in key areas and for the nation to become more self-reliant is a vision that requires one to learn from our own past.

In this regard, I am glad to note that Bhartiya Janta Yuva Morcha, Delhi has compiled a book titled 'Unsung Warriors' commemorating 75 years of India's Independence. This book includes a compilation of stories of unsung heroes who have contributed to our freedom struggle; it attempts to bring more awareness about their contribution among the youth of India.

I congratulate the team of BJYM Delhi. I urge the youth to read this book and inculcate values & learn lessons from the lives & work of our forgotten heroes.

Yours Sincerely

(Tejasvi Surya)

Office Address: #44, 11th Main, Aurobindo Marg, Jayanagar 5th Block,
Opp. Pu ti Na Park, Bengaluru-5600
Phone: 080 26651166 | Email: contact@tejasvisurya.in

भारतीय जनता पार्टी, दिल्ली प्रदेश
Bharatiya Janata Party, Delhi Pradesh

4 अप्रैल, 2023

संदेश

यह जानकर हार्दिक प्रसन्नता हो रही है कि भारतीय जनता युवा मोर्चा दिल्ली प्रदेश द्वारा 'गुमनाम योद्धा' नामक पुस्तक का संयोजन किया जा रहा है।

इसमें स्वतंत्रता के 75 वर्ष पूर्ण होने पर 'अमृत महोत्सव' पर वीर जवानों, देशभक्तों, स्वतंत्रता सेनानियों के बारे में विभिन्न जानकारियाँ समायोजित होंगी। यह आज की युवा पीढ़ी को उनके देश-प्रेम, संघर्ष एवं विचारों से अवगत कराने में अहम भूमिका निभाएगी।

आशा करता हूँ कि संपादक मंडल के अथक प्रयासों से 'गुमनाम योद्धा' के प्रकाशन का उद्देश्य सफल होगा और आज के युवाओं एवं युवतियों के साथ-साथ भाजपा युवा मोर्चा से जुड़े कार्यकर्ताओं के बीच यह लोकप्रिय होगी।

शुभकामनाओं सहित,

भवदीय

(वीरेंद्र सचदेवा)

अध्यक्ष

14, पंडित पंत मार्ग, नई दिल्ली-110001, दूरभाष / फैक्स : 23712323, 23712744, 23712509
14, Pt. Pant Marg, New Delhi- 110001, Telefax: 23712744, 23712323, 23712509
इ-मेल : bjpdelhioffice@gmail.com, वेब : www.bjpdelhi.org

Preface

In today's fast changing world and tough competitive day-to-day life, the youth hardly find time to remember our rich heritage and past. It becomes more important when the country celebrates the Amrit Mahotsav of Independence (commemorating 75 years of Indian independence). The fight against colonial rule in India constitutes a unique narrative, which is not affected by violence. Rather, a narrative that is replete with diverse tales of heroism, bravery, *satyagraha,* dedication and sacrifice across the length and breadth of the subcontinent. These stories make up the rich Indian cultural heritage and traditions. Thus, anonymous warriors need not define lesser-known freedom fighters. Sometimes they can be leaders whose ideals portray the Indian value system.

The section on unsung warriors is an attempt to remember and recall the forgotten heroes of our freedom struggle, many of whom may be famous but are unknown to the new generation. The objective of recreating and bringing to the fore the stories lying in the form of faded memories of the past will become a medium of inspiration and encouragement for the generations to come. India 2.0 is not just about promoting the spirit of India in any one particular paradigm of development. It covers all areas of life; above all it enriches our hearts and souls. The spirit of India is incomplete without remembering and paying gratitude to our unsung heroes. It is our duty to pay homage to them on this journey of growth and development. their ethos and principles should always be remembered and respected.

—Aditi Sharma

Author's Note

We all Indians are impressed by our visionary Prime Minister Shri Narendra Modi. His vision, indomitable will power, strong leadership, big dreams to develop the nation and protection of our traditions, values and by giving us the pledge to celebrate the heritage, he has inspired everyone for nation building. On 15th December, 2021, in his monthly radio programme 'Mann Ki Baat', he emphasised the need to remember the unsung heroes of the 'Indian Independence Movement'. This is the most humble way to pay gratitude to those who dedicated their lives for the integrity of their motherland.

Knowing the importance of this work, our organisation considered me worthy to present the book by compiling material on forgotten warriors, this is my great fortune. It was really a very difficult task, but I have been able to do it with the constant guidance and support of our colleagues and elders. This book is dedicated as a tribute to the innumerable warriors who sacrificed their lives for our freedom.

- 'Salute to their every struggle'
- 'Salute to all their thoughts'

My special thanks to respected Shri Ajayji (Rashtriya

Swayamsevak Sangh, Zonal Intellectual Head, North India Region), who guided me to write this book and take the stories of revolutionaries to the masses, which has been a constant inspiration for this publication. Dr. Vishnu Mittal (Treasurer, B.J.P., Delhi & Co-Incharge, Bharatiya Janata Yuva Morcha, Delhi) helped us to make this effort a success & supported this publication through his NGO 'Aao Saath Chalen'. May this book become a medium to celebrate the glory of the 'Unsung Warriors'. It is a noble duty of our present and future generations to remember their contribution.

—Aditi Sharma

Contents

1

Abadi Bano Begum

(1852 – 13 November, 1920)

Abadi Bano Begum was a prominent voice in the Indian Independence movement. She was also known as Bi Amman. She was one of the first Muslim women to actively take part in politics and was part of the movement to free India from the British Raj.

Born in 1850 in Uttar Pradesh, she married Abdul Ali Khan, a senior official in the Rampur state. The couple had one daughter and five sons. After her husband's death at a young age, the responsibility to look after her children fell on her. Even though she had limited resources, Abadi Bano Begum pawned her personal jewellery to educate her children. Bano Begum did not have any formal education but still sent her children to an English-medium school in the town of Bareilly, Uttar Pradesh. Her sons, Maulana Mohammad Ali Jouhar and Maulana Shaukat Ali went on to become leading figures of the Khilafat movement and the Indian Independence movement. They played an important role during the non-co-operation movement against the British Raj. Abadi Bano Begum took an active part in politics and was part of the Khilafat Committee. In 1917, she joined the agitation to demand release of Annie Besant and her two sons from prison. Mahatma Gandhi encouraged her to speak, as she could muster the support of women in the freedom movement. In 1917, during the sessions of the All India Muslim League, she gave a most touching and forceful speech which left a lasting impression on the Muslims of British India. She travelled extensively throughout India to galvanise support for the Khilafat movement.

Abadi Bano Begum played an important part in fundraising for the Khilafat movement and the Indian Iindependence movement. She, along with Begum Hasrat Mohani, the wife of Maulana Hasrat Mohani, Basanti Devi, Sarala Devi Chaudhurani and Sarojini Naidu often addressed women-only gatherings and exhorted the women to donate to the Tilak Swaraj Fund, which was set up by Bal Gangadhar Tilak for the Indian freedom movement. She was active in the freedom movement until her death in 1924. On 14 August, 1990, Pakistan Post Office issued a commemorative postage stamp in her honour in its 'Pioneers of Freedom' series.

Abadi Bano Begum died on 13 November, 1920 at the age of seventy-three.

□

2

Abdul Qaiyum Ansari

(1 July, 1905 – 18 January, 1973)

Abdul Qaiyum Ansari was a participant in the freedom struggle of India. He was known for his commitment to national integration, secularism and communal harmony. He was a leader who worked against the demand of Muslim league for creation of a separate Muslim nation from India into an independent State. He fought against Jinnah's two-nation theory through All India Momin Conference of which he was the president.

Birth and Education

Ansari born on 1 July, 1905 at Dehri-on-Sone, Bihar. He was born in a wealthy Momin/Ansari family. After studying at Sasaram and Dehri-on-Sone High Schools, he went on to attend the Aligarh Muslim University, Calcutta University and Allahabad University, though his education was interrupted from time to time due to his active involvement in the struggle for India's freedom.

Freedom Struggle in India

Abdul Ansari was involved in the freedom struggle at a very early age and as a part of the same he left the government-run school at his home town. He established a national school for the students who had boycotted government schools in response to the call of the Indian National Congress. For this, he was arrested and imprisoned at the young age of 16 since it amounted to participation in non-co-operation and Khilafat movements.

He worked closely with the Indian National Congress as a youth leader and even took part in the students' agitation against the Simon Commission during its visit to Calcutta in 1928.

Abdul Qaiyum Ansari was also an accomplished journalist, writer and poet. He was editor of Urdu weekly *Al-Islah* (The Reform) and an Urdu monthly *Musawat* (Equality) in the pre-Independence days.

Post Independence

During the aggression by Pakistan on Kashmir in October 1947, he came forward as the first Muslim leader of India to condemn the same and strenuously worked to rouse the Muslim masses to counter such aggressions as true citizens of India. As an aftermath of this he founded the Indian Muslim Youth Kashmir Front in 1957 to 'liberate' Azad Kashmir. Later on, he exhorted the Indian Muslims to support the Government of India in the anti-Indian uprising of the Razakars in Hyderabad, during September 1948.

A champion of the poor and downtrodden, Abdul Qaiyum Ansari worked for the spread of education and literacy and the first All India Backward Classes Commission was appointed by the Government of India in 1953, largely at his initiative.

Death

Abdul Qaiyum Ansari died on 18 January, 1973, at village Amiawar of Bihar, while inspecting damages caused to the village by the collapse of the Dehri-Arrah canal and organising relief for its homeless people.

□

3
Ahmad Saeed Dehlavi

(1888 – 4 December, 1959)

Ahmad Saeed Dehlavi was an Indian Muslim scholar and freedom struggle activist who served as the first general secretary and the fifth president of Jamiat Ulama-e-Hind. He also served as the third rector of Madrasa Aminia and authored books such as Fear of Hell and Key to the Garden of Bliss.

Ahmad Saeed Dehlavi in 1888 in Daryaganj, Delhi. He received his primary education from Abdul Majeed Mustafabadi and Muhammad Yasin Sikandarabadi, and memorized the Quran at Madrasa Hussainia in Delhi. He entered Madrasa Aminia in 1328 AH and graduated in 1336 AH. His teachers included Kifayatullah Dehlawi.

Saeed participated in the Indian freedom struggle and was imprisoned eight times. He was arrested in 1921 and jailed in the Central Jail Mianwali for one year. He was arrested for the last time in 1942 and imprisoned in the jails of Delhi, Lahore, Ferozpur and Multan. He was among the founders of the Jamiat Ulama-e-Hind (JUH) and was appointed the interim secretary in the meeting of inception in November 1919.

Saeed was appointed the first general secretary of the JUH in November 1920, a position he served for twenty years. He served as the vice-president of the JUH for seventeen years from 1940 to 1957. He taught at the Madrasa Aminia and was appointed its rector in 1953 following the death of Kifayatullah Dehlawi. He served as the president of the JUH for two years from 1957 until his death on 4 December 1959 in Delhi.Saeed was seen as an influential speaker. He was known as Sahbān al-Hind. In September 2019, JUH organized a two-days seminar on the life and works of Saeed. It was attended by scholars and poets including Akhtarul Wasey, Gulzar Dehlvi and Usman Mansoorpuri.

□

4

Ahmadullah Shah

(1787–5 June, 1858)

Ahmadullah Shah, famous as Maulvi of Faizabad, freedom fighter and a leader of the Indian revolt of 1857, was known as the 'lighthouse of rebellion' in Awadh region. British officers, like George Bruce Malleson and Thomas Seaton have mentioned about the courage, valour and personal and organisational capabilities of Ahmadullah. G.B. Malleson repeatedly mentions in the *History of Indian Mutiny*, a book written in six volumes, covers the Indian revolt of 1857. Thomas Seaton describes Ahmadullah Shah as a man of great abilities, undaunted courage, stern determination and by far the best soldier among the rebels.

Being a practicing Muslim, he was also an epitome of religious unity and Ganga-Jamuna culture of Faizabad. In the rebellion of 1857, royalties like Nana Sahib and Khan Bahadur Khan fought alongside Ahmadullah.

The British could never catch the Maulvi alive. The

price of 50,000 pieces of silver was announced to capture him. Finally the king of Powayan, Raja Jagannath Singh killed the Maulvi, beheaded and presented his head to the British for which the king was paid the announced prize. Next day, the head of Maulvi was hung at the *kotwali*.

Arrest at Patna

According to G.B. Malleson, when the Maulvi was in Patna, suddenly with no previous notice or intimation, an officer arrived at Patna from Punjab. He is referred as Lt. Thursbern in a book by Rashmi Kumari on Ahmadullah Shah. With a warrant in his pocket, he walked into Sadikpur, a quarter in Patna. He entered the house of Ahmadullah Shah and with the help of the police arrested Maulvi Ahmadullah Shah.[5] The Maulvi was awarded capital death punishment on charges of revolt and conspiracy against the British rule. The punishment was later reduced to life imprisonment.

After eruption of revolt on 10 May, 1857, the rebel sepoys of Azamgarh, Benaras and Jaunpur reached Patna on June 7. They attacked the bungalows of English officers who were already on the run. Once the city was captured by the rebels, they took charge of the government treasury. They proceeded towards the jail and got Maulvi and other prisoners freed. After declaring Mansingh as Raja of Patna, Maulvi Ahmadullah proceeded to Awadh.

Indian Rebellion of 1857 and 1858

The rebel army of Awadh was led by Barkat Ahmad and Maulvi Ahmadullah Shah. In the battle of Chinhat, Barkat Ahmad was declared Chief Army Officer of the rebels. The British Army was led by Henry Montgomery

Lawrence, who eventually died at the Residency, Lucknow. This fierce battle was won by the rebel army under the leadership of Barkat Ahmad and Maulvi Ahmadullah Shah.

Ahmadullah Shah also led an attack on Beligarad. The writer Kaisaruttawarikh states that it was a huge victory for the rebels. Maulvi fought with great courage and chivalry in the real sense and for that he succeeded in pushing the British to Beligarad. Subsequently the big building of Machchhi Bhavan was blown up.

After Lucknow was captured by the rebels, Birjis Qadr, the 10-year-old son of Wazid Ali Shah and Begum Hazrat Mahal was declared the king. Maulvi resisted being part of the new administration. He went away from the palace politics and established his camp with Ghamandi Singh and 1,000 soldiers of Subedar Umrao Singh at Badshah Bagh, beyond River Gomati.

On 6 March, 1858, the British attacked Lucknow again under the leadership of Sir Colin Campbell, a reputed British Army official. The rebel army was led by Begum Hazrat Mahal. With the capture of Lucknow by the British, the rebels escaped on March 15 and 16 through a road leading to Faizabad. The last rebels, that is, 1,200 men under Ahmadullah Shah were driven from a fortified house in the centre of the city on March 21. The city was declared cleared on this date.

After the fall of Lucknow, Maulvi shifted his base to Shahjahanpur, Rohilkhand. In Shahjahanpur, forces of Nana Sahib and Khan Bahadur Khan also joined Maulvi in attacking the British.

Colin Campbell departed from Shahjahanpur on May 2 towards Bareilly. Maulvi, with King of Mohammadi and several thousand soldiers attacked Shahjahanpur.

The British Army was informed and General Brigadier John reached Shahjahanpur on May 11. Jones could not muster enough courage to attack Maulvi and kept waiting for more assistance from Bareilly. George Bruce Malleson writes:

"Maulvi was the only one who could have dared to defeat Sir Colin Campbell twice."

The fierce battle took place on 15 May, 1858 between platoon of rebels and regiment of General Brigadier Jones. Both sides had to bear heavy losses but the rebels still controlled Shahjahanpur. Colin reached Shahjahanpur on May 20 and attacked Shahjahanpur from all sides. This battle continued all night long. Maulvi and Nana Sahib left Shahjahanpur. It is said that Colin himself pursued Maulvi but couldn't capture him. After the fall of Shahjahanpur, Maulvi left for Powayan which was situated 18 miles north of Shahjahanpur.

Death

The British could never catch Maulvi alive. They announced 50,000 pieces of silver as prize to capture him. Maulvi wanted to induce the king of Powayan, Raja Jagannath Singh to revolt against the British, but the latter did not relent to Maulvi's wishes. When Maulvi reached gates of his palace on his war elephant, the king attacked him by firing a cannon shot. This killed Maulvi who dropped down from his elephant. G.B. Malleson describes his death thus: "Thus died the Moulvee Ahmed Oolah Shah of Faizabad. If a patriot is a man who plots and fights for independence, wrongfully destroyed, for his native country, then most certainly, the Moulvee was a true patriot."

Kunwar Baldeo Singh, brother of the king of Powayan, Raja Jagannath Singh killed Maulvi Ahmadullah Shah by beheading him and presenting his head to the magistrate. He was paid the announced prize and found favour with the British. The head of Maulvi was hanged at the *kotwali* next day. Another revolutionary of 1857, Fazl-e-Haq Khairabadi, witnessed the death of Maulvi.

□

5

Alekh Patra

(1 July, 1923 – 17 November, 1999)

Alekh Patra was a prominent leader of Indian nationalism in British-ruled India. Employing non-violent civil disobedience, he participated in the Indian Independence struggle and inspired movements for civil rights, environmental protection and civil rights across different regions of Orissa. He participated in the freedom movement at the age of about eighteen. During the course of the freedom struggle, he, along with his friends, burnt down the police station at Nimapada in protest against British Raj. During this event, there was police firing and one of his close associates and friends died on the spot. He survived and was arrested and put in Puri Jail. He continued his underground struggle against colonialism. He went to Calcutta and worked there as a domestic help in a rich man's house, continuing with underground activities..

But he could not stay long there as he wanted to fight openly with Acharya Harihar, Gopabandhu Das, etc. and on request of his friends, he came back to Orissa. He was caught at the Puri Railway Station when he returned Calcutta and again put into jail.

Inside the jail, he practicised cotton spinning in order

to produce his own clothes, cleaned toilets to maintain a hygienic environment, did daily group prayers and followed all the other instructions of Gandhiji. After being released from jail, he went to Wardha to get training on *swaraj*, Home Rule and other *Sarvodaya* works.

He was awarded the freedom fighter's pension, copper honorarium by the Government of India, honorarium from the Citizen's Forum of Kashipur for the cause of environment and tribal people's cause and a certified letter of perfection in *khadi* production by Gandhiji.

□

6

Alluri Sitarama Raju

(15 May, 1897 – 7 May, 1924)

Alluri Sitarama Raju was an Indian revolutionary involved in the Indian Independence movement. After the passing of the 1882 Madras Forest Act, its restrictions on the free movement of tribals in the forest prevented them from engaging in their traditional *podu* agricultural system, which involved shifting cultivation. Alluri led the Rampa Rebellion of 1922, during which a band of tribals and other sympathisers fought in the border areas of the East Godavari and Visakhapatnam regions of Madras Presidency, in present-day Andhra Pradesh, against the British Raj, which had passed the law. He was referred to as 'Manyam Veerudu' by the local people.

Harnessing some aspects of the earlier non-co-operation movement and with widespread support among the tribal people, Alluri led raids on police stations in and around Chintapalle, Rampachodavaram,

Dammanapalli, Krishna Devi Peta, Rajavommangi, Addateegala, Narsipatnam and Annavaram. With his followers, he stole guns and ammunition and killed several British police officers, including two near Dammanapalli. Alluri was eventually trapped by the British in the forests of Chintapalle, then tied to a tree and executed by gunfire in Koyyuru village. His tomb is in Krishnadevipeta village.

Alluri adopted aspects of the Gandhian non-co-operation movement, such as promoting temperance and boycott of colonial courts in favour of local justice administered by Panchayat courts, to attract support. Although the movement died out in early 1922, it had reached the plains and he was involved in propagation of some of its methods among the hill people as a means to raise their political consciousness and desire for change. It was these actions that caused him to be put under police surveillance from around February of that year, although the fact that he was using them as a camouflage to foment armed uprising seems not to have been recognised by either the movement's political leadership or the British. The armed rebellion began in August when Alluri led a mob of 500 people in looting, on consecutive days, of police stations at Chintapalle, Krishna Devi Peta and Rajavommangi, from where he acquired guns and ammunition. He subsequently toured the area to rope in more recruits and killed a member of a British police force that had been sent to find him.

The British struggled in their pursuit, in part because of the unfamiliar terrain and also because the local people in this sparsely-populated area were generally unwilling to help them and often outrightly keen to materially assist Alluri besides providing shelter and intelligence. While based in the hills, contemporary official reports suggested that the core group of rebels dwindled to between 80 and 100 but this figure rose dramatically whenever they moved to take action against the British because of the involvement of people in the villages.

Further deaths occurred on September 23 when Alluri ambushed a police party from a high position as they were going through the Dammanapalli Ghat, killing two officers and cementing his reputation among the disaffected people. There were further two successful attacks against the police forces during the month, after which the British realised that his style of guerrilla warfare would have to be matched with a similar response, for which they drafted in members of the Special Malabar Police, who were trained in such methods.

Attempts to persuade the local people to inform on or withdraw their support to Alluri, through both incentives and reprisals, did nothing but encourage them to further their actions.[4] Further raids were later made on police stations at Rampachodavaram, Addateegala, Narsipatnam and Annavaram.

Alluri was eventually trapped by the British in the forests of Chintapalle. He was tied to a tree and shot dead in Koyyuru village. His tomb is in Krishna Devi Peta village.

□

7

Amir Chand Bombwal

(8 August, 1893 – 10 February, 1972)

Bombwal was born in Punjab. He was a journalist, a freedom fighter in the Indian Independence movement, a Khudai Khidmatgar and a political leader of the Indian National Congress Party from Peshawar, North-West Frontier Province (NWFP) of British India. He was the founder, editor and publisher of a weekly newspaper, *The Frontier Mail* and a close associate of Khan Abdul Ghaffar Khan whom, it has been claimed, he named 'Frontier Gandhi'.

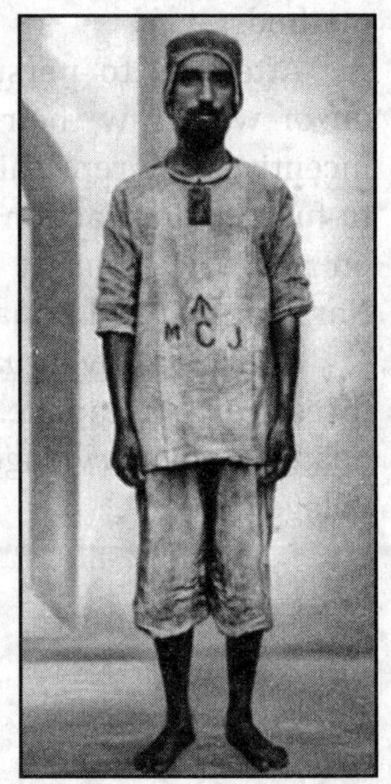

Bombwal was the last editor of the short lived Urdu-language *Swarajya* weekly newspaper, published between 1907 and 1911 by the Bharat Mata Society in Allahabad. This newspaper pursued a scathing campaign against British Raj rule. An active member of the Indian National Congress Party, he was jailed for participation in the first Non-Co-operation Movement in 1921-23

Upon release from jail, he worked to rehabilitate the refugees and victims of the 1924 Kohat riots. Mahatma Gandhi commended him for the service he provided to the riot victims.

After the Partition of India, he was arrested without charges, along with Khan Abdul Ghaffar Khan and Khan Abdul Jabbar Khan (known as Khan Sahib) by the founder of Pakistan, Mohammed Ali Jinnah, who suspected them of undermining the accession of N-WFP to Pakistan.

They were jailed in Peshawar Central Jail and there was little hope of their release. Upon the death of Jinnah, Liaquat Ali Khan, who was on friendly terms with them, assumed the reins of power in Pakistan. Liaquat Ali Khan facilitated their release from jail and transferred Bombwal to India, in 1948, where he arrived on a flight carrying the ceasefire delegation of the Indo-Pakistani war of 1947 from Pakistan.

After Partition, he settled down in Dehradun in India and continued to publish *The Frontier Mail* from there. He gave the Indian people a floor-to-ceiling height oil painting of Vithalbhai Patel that now hangs on right side of the dais in Central Hall of the Indian Parliament.

He died in Delhi of natural causes. Upon his death, fifteen trunks containing his documents were transferred to the National Archives of India.

□

8

Ananta Singh

(1 December, 1903 – 25 January, 1979)

Ananta Singh was an Indian revolutionary, who participated in the Chittagong armoury raid in 1930. Later, he founded a far-Left radical communist group, called the Revolutionary Communist Council of India.

The role of Singh was played by actor Maninder Singh in the 2010 Hindi film, '*Khelein Hum Jee Jaan Sey*' and actor Jaideep Ahlawat in the 2012 film, '*Chittagong*'. Singh's involvement in the Indian nationalist movement began with the non-co-operation movement, in 1921. Although he incited his schoolmates to join the movement, he personally did not have much faith in the movement. On 14 December, 1923, he and Nirmal Sen led the robbery at the treasury office of the Assam Bengal Railway according to the plan made by Surya Sen and clashed with the police after the robbery on December 24. He fled from the scene after the robbery and reached Calcutta after a short stay at Sandwip. He was arrested in Calcutta but released soon.

He was again arrested in 1924 and imprisoned for four years.

After his release, he founded a gymnasium and recruited many youths for the revolutionary movement led by Surya Sen. On 18 April, 1930, he was one of the leaders of the Chittagong armoury raid. After the incident, he was able to flee from Chittagong with Ganesh Ghosh and Jiban Ghoshal. After a short encounter with the police at Feni Railway Station, he took shelter in the French territory, Chandernagore. But, on hearing the news of the torture faced by his fellow revolutionaries who were already in jail, he surrendered to the police on 28 June, 1930 at Calcutta and faced the trial. In the trial, he was sentenced to transportation for life to the Cellular Jail in Port Blair. After a long hunger strike in the Cellular Jail in 1932, he was brought back to a mainland jail, along with a number of his fellow political prisoners due to the initiative of Mahatma Gandhi and Rabindranath Tagore. After his final release in 1946, he joined the Communist Party of India.

Singh's most significant work is his controversial autobiography, *Keu Bale Dakat, Keu Bale Biplabi* (Some Call Me a Robber, Some Call Me a Revolutionary). His other significant works include: *Chattagram Yubabidroha* (Youth Revolution in Chittagong) (in two volumes), *Agnigarbha Chattagram* (Chittagong on Fire), *Masterda on Surya Sen, Surya Sener Svapna O Sadhana* (Dream and Austerities of Surya Sen) and *Ami Sei Meye* (I am that Girl). Between 1960 and 1966, he even produced three Bengali films, including the hit '*Jamalaye Jibanta Manush*'.

□

9

Annie Besant

(1 October, 1847 – 20 September, 1933)

Annie Besant was a British socialist, theosophist, women's rights activist, writer, orator, educationist and philanthropist. Regarded as a champion of human freedom, she was an ardent supporter of both Irish and Indian self-rule. She was a prolific author with over three hundred books and pamphlets to her credit. As an educationist, her contributions included being one of the founders of the Benaras Hindu University.

For Besant, politics, friendship and love were always closely intertwined. Her decision in favour of socialism stemmed from her close relationship with George Bernard Shaw, a struggling young Irish author living in London and a leading light of the Fabian Society and who considered Besant to be 'the greatest orator in England'. Annie was impressed by his work and grew very close to him in the early 1880s. It was Besant who made the first move by inviting Shaw to live with her. This he refused, but it was Shaw who sponsored Besant to join the Fabian

Society. In its early days, the Society was a gathering of people exploring spiritual, rather than political, alternatives to the capitalist system. Besant began to write for the Fabians. This new commitment – and her relationship with Shaw – deepened the split between Besant and Bradlaugh, who was an individualist and opposed to socialism of any sort. While he defended free speech at any cost, he was very cautious about encouraging working-class militancy. Unemployment was a central issue of the time and in 1887, some of the London's unemployed started to hold protests at Trafalgar Square. Besant agreed to appear as a speaker at a meeting on November 13. The police tried to stop the assembly, fighting broke out and troops were called in. Many were hurt, one man died, and hundreds were arrested; Besant offered herself for arrest – an offer disregarded by the police.

The events created a great sensation and became known as 'Bloody Sunday'. Besant was widely blamed – or credited – for it. She threw herself into organising legal aid for the jailed workers and support for their families. Bradlaugh finally broke with her because he felt she should have asked his advice before going ahead with the meeting.

Another activity in this period was her involvement in the London match-girls' strike of 1888. She was drawn into this battle of the 'New Unionism' by a young socialist, Herbert Burrows. He had made contact with workers at Bryant and May's match factory in Bow, London. They were mainly young women and were very poorly paid. They were also prey to industrial illnesses, like the bone-rotting Phossy jaw, which was caused by the chemicals used in match manufacture. Some of the match workers asked for help from Burrows and Besant in establishing a union.

Besant met the women and set up a committee, which led the women to strike for better pay and conditions – an action that won public support. Besant led demonstrations by 'match-girls', who were cheered on the streets and prominent churchmen wrote in their support. In just over a week, they forced the firm to improve pay and conditions. Besant then helped them to set up a proper union and a social centre.

At the time, the match-stick industry was a very powerful lobby, since electric light was not yet widely available and matches were an essential commodity; in 1872, lobbyists from the match industry persuaded the British Government to change its planned tax policy. Besant's campaign was the first time anyone had successfully challenged the match manufacturers on a major issue, and was seen as a landmark victory in the early years of British socialism.

In 1884, Besant developed a very close friendship with Edward Aveling, a young socialist teacher who lived in her house for a time. Aveling was a scholarly figure and it was he who first translated the important works of Marx into English. He eventually went to live with Eleanor Marx, daughter of Karl Marx. Aveling was a great influence on Besant's thinking and she supported his work, yet she moved towards the rival Fabians at that time. Aveling and Eleanor Marx had joined the Marxist Social Democratic Federation and then the Socialist League, a small Marxist splinter group which formed around the artist, William Morris.

It seems that Morris played a large part in converting Besant to Marxism, but it was to the SDF, not his Socialist League, that she turned in 1888. She remained a member for a number of years and became one of its best speakers. She was still a member of the Fabian Society; neither she nor anyone else seemed to think the two movements to be incompatible at the time. Soon after joining the Marxists, Besant was elected to the London School Board in 1888. Women at that time were not able to take part in parliamentary politics, but had been brought into the local electorate in 1881. Besant drove about with a red ribbon in her hair, speaking at meetings. "No more hungry children," her manifesto proclaimed. She combined her socialist principles with feminism: "I ask the electors to vote for me, and the non-electors to work for me because women are wanted on the Board and there are too few women candidates." Besant came out on top of the poll in Tower Hamlets, with over 15,000 votes. She wrote in the *National Reformer*: "Ten years ago, under a cruel law, Christian bigotry robbed me of my little child. Now the care of the 763,680 children of London is placed partly in my hands."

As early as 1902 Besant had written that "India is not ruled for the prosperity of the people, but rather for the profit of her conquerors, and her sons are being treated as a conquered race." She encouraged Indian national consciousness, attacked caste and child marriage and worked effectively for Indian education. Along with her theosophical activities, Besant continued to actively participate in political matters. She joined the Indian National Congress. As the name suggested, this was originally a debating body, which met each year to consider resolutions on political issues; mostly it demanded more of a say for middle-class Indians in British Indian government. It had not yet developed into a permanent mass movement with local organisation. About this time her co-worker Leadbeater moved to Sydney.

In 1914, World War I broke out and Britain asked for support of its Empire in the fight against Germany. Echoing an Irish nationalist slogan, Besant declared, "England's need is India's opportunity." As editor of the *New India* newspaper, she attacked the colonial government of India and called for clear and decisive moves towards self-rule. As with Ireland, the government refused to discuss any changes while the war lasted. In 1916, Besant launched the All India Home Rule League along with Lokmanya Tilak, once again modelling the demands for India on Irish nationalist practices. This was the first political party in India to have regime change as its main goal. Unlike the Congress itself, the League worked all the year round. It built a structure of local branches, enabling it to mobilise demonstrations, public meetings and agitations. In June 1917, Besant was arrested and interned at a hill station, where she defiantly flew a red and green flag. The Congress and the Muslim League together threatened to launch protests if she were not set free; Besant's arrest had created a focus for protest. The government was forced to give way and to make vague but significant concessions. It was announced that the ultimate aim of British rule was Indian self-government, and moves in that direction were promised. Besant was freed in September 1917, welcomed by crowds all over India and in December, she took over as president of the Indian National Congress for a year. Both Jawaharlal Nehru and Mahatma Gandhi spoke of Besant's influence with admiration.

After the war, a new leadership of the Indian National Congress emerged around Mahatma Gandhi, one of those to have written for Besant's release. He was a lawyer who had returned from leading Asians in a peaceful struggle against racism in South Africa. Jawaharlal Nehru, Gandhi's closest collaborator, had been educated by a theosophist tutor. The new leadership was committed to action that was both militant and non-violent, but there were differences between them and Besant. Despite her past, she was not happy with their socialist leanings. Until the end of her life, however, she continued to campaign for India's Independence, not only in India but also on speaking tours of Britain. In her own version of Indian dress, she remained a striking presence on speakers' platforms. She produced a torrent of letters and articles demanding Independence.

Besant tried as a person, theosophist and president of the Theosophical Society to accommodate Krishnamurti's views ino her life without success; she vowed to personally follow him in his new direction although she apparently had trouble understanding both his motives and his new message.The two remained friends until the end of her life. In 1931, she fell ill in India. Besant died on 20 September, 1933, at age 85, in Adyar, Madras Presidency. Her body was cremated.

□

10

Aruna Asaf Ali

(16 July, 1909 – 29 July, 1996)

Aruna Asaf Ali was an Indian educator, political activist and publisher. As an active participant in the Indian Independence movement, she is widely remembered for hoisting the Indian national flag at the Gowalia Tank Maidan in Bombay during the Quit India movement in 1942. Post Independence, she remained active in politics and became Delhi's first Mayor.

Aruna Asaf Ali was born (Aruna Ganguly) on 16 July, 1909 in Kalka, Punjab (now in Haryana) in a Bengali Brahmo Samaj family. Her father Upendranath Ganguly hailed from Barisal district of East Bengal (now Bangladesh) but settled in the United Provinces. He was a restaurant owner. Her mother Ambalika Devi was the daughter of Trailokyanath Sanyal, a renowned Brahmo Samaj leader who wrote many Brahmo hymns. Upendranath Ganguly's younger brother Dhirendranath Ganguly was one of the earliest film directors. Another brother, Nagendranath, was a university professor who married Nobel Prize-winner Rabindranath Tagore's only surviving daughter Mira Devi. Aruna's sister, Purnima Banerjee, was a member of the Constituent Assembly of India.

Aruna was educated at Sacred Heart Convent in Lahore and then at All Saints' College in Nainital. After her graduation, she worked as a teacher at the Gokhale Memorial School in Calcutta. She met Asaf Ali, a leader in the Congress Party, at Allahabad. They got married in 1928 despite parental opposition on grounds of religion and age (he was a Muslim and her senior by more than 20 years).

Aruna Asaf Ali played a major role in the Indian Independence movement. She became a member of the Indian National Congress after marrying Asaf Ali and participated in public processions during the Salt Satyagraha. She was arrested on the charge that she was a vagrant and hence was not released in 1931 under the Gandhi-Irwin Pact which stipulated release of all political prisoners. Other women co-prisoners refused to leave the premises unless she was also released, but gave in only after Mahatma Gandhi intervened. A public agitation secured her release.

In 1932, she was held prisoner in the Tihar Jail where she protested against the indifferent treatment meted out to political prisoners by goiong on a hunger strike. Her efforts resulted in an improvement in the conditions inside the Tihar Jail, but she was moved to Ambala and subjected to solitary confinement. She was politically not very active after her release, but at the end of 1942, she took part in the underground movement as an active participant. .

Rise to Prominence during the Quit India Movement

On 8 August, 1942, the All India Congress Committee passed the Quit India resolution at the Bombay session. The British government responded by arresting all major leaders and members of the Congress Working Committee, thus pre-empting the movement from success. Young Aruna Asaf Ali presided over the remainder of the session on August 9 and hoisted the Congress flag at the Gowalia Tank Maidan. This marked the commencement of the movement. The police fired upon the assembly at the session. Aruna was dubbed the 'heroine of the 1942 movement' for her bravery in the face of danger and was called the 'Grand Old Lady of the Independence Movement' in her later years. Despite the absence of direct leadership, spontaneous protests and demonstrations were held all over the country as an expression of the desire of India's youth to achieve Independence.

An arrest warrant was issued in her name but she went underground to evade arrest and started an underground movement in the year 1942. Her property was seized and sold. Meanwhile, she also edited *Inquilab*, a monthly magazine of the Congress Party, along with Ram Manohar Lohia. In the 1944 issue, she exhorted the youth to action by asking them to forget futile discussions about violence and non-violence and join the revolution. Leaders, such as Jayaprakash Narayan and Aruna Asaf Ali were described as 'the political children of Gandhi but recent students of Karl Marx.' The government announced a reward of 5,000 rupees for her capture. She fell ill and for a period hid in Dr Joshi's hospital at Karol Bagh in Delhi. Mahatma Gandhi sent her a hand-written note advising her to come out of hiding and surrender herself as her mission had been accomplished and as she could utilise the reward amount for the Harijan cause. However, she came out of hiding only after the warrant against her was withdrawn in 1946. She treasured the note from the Mahatma and it adorned her drawing room. However, she also faced criticism from Gandhi for her support of the Royal Indian Navy Mutiny, a movement she saw as the single greatest unifying factor of Hindus and Muslims when the demand for forming Pakistan was at its peak.

Post-Independence Mayorship and Career in Publishing

Aruna was a member of the Congress Socialist Party, a caucus within the Congress Party for activists with socialist leanings. Disillusioned with the progress of the Congress Party on socialism, she joined a new party, the Socialist Party, in 1948. She, however, left that party along with Edatata Narayanan and they visited Moscow along with Rajani Palme Dutt. Both of them joined the Communist Party of India in the early 1950s. On the personal front, she was bereaved when Asaf Ali died in 1953.

In 1954, she helped form the National Federation of Indian Women, the women's wing of CPI but left the party in 1956, following Nikita Khrushchev's disowning of Stalin. In 1958, she was elected the first Mayor of Delhi. She was closely associated with social activists and secularists of her era, like Krishna Menon, Vimla Kapoor, Guru Radha Kishan, Premsagar Gupta, Rajani Palme Dutt, Sarla Sharma and Subhadra Joshi who were engaged in social welfare and development, in Delhi.

She and Narayanan started the Link publishing house and published a daily newspaper, *Patriot* and a weekly, *Link* the same year. The publications became prestigious due to the patronage of leaders like Jawaharlal Nehru, Krishna Menon and Biju Patnaik. Later she moved out of the publishing house due to internal politics and disheartened at the greed of her comrades. Despite reservations about the Emergency, she remained close to Indira Gandhi and Rajiv Gandhi.

Later she died at New Delhi on 29 July, 1996, aged 87.

□

11

Atulkrishna Ghosh

(1890 – 4 May, 1966)

Atulkrishna Ghosh was an Indian revolutionary, member of the Anushilan Samiti and a leader of the Jugantar movement which was involved in Hindu-German conspiracy during World War I.

Atul was born in 1890, in a Bengali Hindu middle-class Kayastha family of the Jaduboyra-Etmampur village in Kushtia sub-division, which was then in Nadia district, now in Bangladesh. His parents were Taresh Chandra and Binodini Devi. Atul had to interrupt his studies for his political commitment. The college and its hostel were humming with his radical associates, all future celebrities, mostly in scientific research, like Satyendra Nath Bose, Meghnad Saha, Jnan Ghosh, Jnan Mukherjee, Sishir Mitra, Sushil Acharya, Sailen Ghosh, Harish Simha, Jatin Sheth, Hiralal Ray.

Since 1906, with his cousin Nolini Kanta Kar, Atul had been frequenting Jatindranath Mukherjee (Bagha Jatin), who was their neighbour in Kushtia sub-division.

They both entered the local Anushilan Samiti. W. Sealy in his report notes: "Atul Ghosh and Nolini Kanta Kar, two dangerous and important absconders of the gun-running conspiracy" (p. 23). At Calcutta, thanks to Jatin, they both became very close to Sri Aurobindo. While Nolini practiced wrestling with Kikkar Singh, Atul became an expert trainer in self-defence at the Pataldanga branch of the Anushilan Samiti: Atul Krishna Ghosh and Jatindranath Mukherjee founded the Pathuriaghata Byoam Samiti, which was an important centre for armed revolution in Indian national movement. He came across a number of revolutionaries, including Sachin Sanyal's Benares group and Biren Datta Gupta, whom he recommended to Jatindranath. Biren received from the latter, in January 1910, the mandate to assassinate Samsul Alam, Deputy Superintendent of Police, who was manhandling the under-trial prisoners of the Alipore Bomb Case. In connection with Biren's successful mission, Jatindranath with forty-six associates was placed on trial in the Howrah Conspiracy Case. Inside the prison, Jatindranath learnt from his emissaries abroad that Germany was preparing for war against Great Britain.

After his release in 1911, Jatindranath suspended all extremist activities, left Calcutta under the responsibility of Atul, himself forging a grand federation of regional units in the districts. A relentless organiser, Atul sheltered revolutionaries from various units as much in his parents' house at Jaduboyra, as at the Calcuitta residence of Meghamala and K.P. Basu, at 11 Mahendra Gossain's Lane, where there was a free dormitory with homely meals. Even leaders of rival parties, like Pratul

Ganguli of Dacca admit having enjoyed this hospitality at great expense and risk on Atul's side: "We became great friends with Atulkrishna and had confidence in him. I have very often been to his Darjipara residence and spent nights there. He had grown intimate with several of our members, almost close friends. We considered him to be, somewhat, our own colleague and he sincerely hoped to unite our parties so that we could all work together. Frankly speaking, it was thanks to his wish that I met Jatin Mukherjee...Disappointed by the duplicity of the Dacca branch, some of its important workers, however, like Sachin Sanyal and Nagen (Girija) Datta, severed their connection with it and, introduced by Atulkrishna, worked with Rash Behari Bose in Upper India." Atul's elder brother Aghorenath, a civil surgeon, often looked after the bullet wounds received by the patriots.

After the end of the war, Surendranath Banerjee, followed by Barin Ghose and Motilal Roy, successfully negotiated the withdrawal of warrants against the fugitives accused of the Indo-German plot. Atul was adamant in obtaining a promise on certain points: (a) there would be no question of surrendering arms; (b) no questions would be raised on their past activities; (c) no parole would be demanded concerning their future conduct. Atul came out in 1921, but his Dada's (Jatin Mukherjee's) heroic death, "had knocked out his revolutionary ardour and he gave up active politics." Yet, in January 1924, when Gopinath Saha killed an Englishman, mistaking him to be Tegart, the much-hated Commissioner of Calcutta Police (reputed to have shot Jatin Mukherjee dead), .Atul was made a state-prisoner, to be released in 1926. The same year he married

Menokarani Rakshit of Majilpur and took to business, dissociating himself completely from politics. They had no issues. In an interview with Prithwindra Mukherjee (Bagha Jatin's grandson), on 27 October, 1963 – shortly before his death, Atul sighed: "Dada was a magnet; we all, iron scraps, received our energy from him. When he was no more, we all became iron scraps. I still do not know whether my first allegiance went to Dada, or to the motherland."

Asked about the source of Jatindranath's tremendous force, Atul replied: "He was a very well-trained wrestler and an all-round sportsman. But what characterised him was his soul force and his power of concentration. He could pin-point all his energy to a single part of his body, for instance, his fist. A single blow from that fist was equivalent to an electric charge of God knows how many volts!"

Atul died peacefully in his Calcutta residence on 4 May, 1966.

□

12

Baba Khadak Singh

(6 June, 1867 – 6 October, 1963)

Baba Khadak Singh was an Indian playwright, born at Sialkot in British India. He was involved in the Indian Independence movement and was president of the Central Sikh League. He was a Sikh political leader and virtually the first president of the Shiromani Gurdwara Parbandhak Committee. He was among the first batch of students who graduated (1889) from Punjab University, Lahore. His father, Rai Bahadur Sardar Hari Singh, was a wealthy contractor and industrialist. Today, a prominent road, which is a radial road of Connaught Place, New Delhi leading towards Gurdwara Bangla Sahib, is named Baba Kharak Singh Marg, after him.

Kharak Singh, having passed his matriculation examination from Mission High School and intermediate from Murray College, both at Sialkot and after graduating from University of the Punjab (Lahore), joined the Law College at Allahabad. But the death of his father and elder brother in quick succession, interrupted his studies as he had to return to Sialkot to manage the family property.

He started his public life in 1912 as chairman of the reception committee of the 5th session of the Sikh Educational Conference held at Sialkot.

Three years later, in 1915, as president of the 8th session of the conference held at Tarn Taran, he surprised everyone by walking to the site of the conference, breaking the stately custom of arriving in a carriage pulled by six horses. He also refused permission for a proposed resolution to be moved at the conference wishing victory to the British in World War I.

The Jallianwala Bagh massacre of 1919 galvanised Kharak Singh as the virtual core of Sikh politics. He presided over the historic session of the Central Sikh League held in Lahore in 1920 where, under his direction, the Sikhs took part in the non-co-operation movement. Mahatma Gandhi, the Ali brothers and Saifuddin Kitchlew also attended the event and advised the Sikhs to throw in their lot with the Congress Party.

In 1921-22, he successfully led the first *morcha* (agitation) against the British government (November, 1921), which is popularly known as the Keys Morcha. This was a Sikh protest requiring the return of the keys of the *toshakhana* (treasury) of the Golden Temple, which had been seized by the British Deputy Commissioner of Amritsar. Kharak Singh was among the first to be arrested and this was the first of his numerous jail terms under the British. His arrest led to a vigorous storm of protests against the government.

He was jailed on 26 November, 1921 for making an anti-government speech and sentenced to six months' imprisonment on 2 December, 1921. He was released on 17 January, 1922 when the keys of the *toshakhana* were also surrendered to him. In the same year, he was elected president of the Punjab Provincial Congress Committee.

Babaji was, however, rearrested soon and, on 4 April, 1922, he was awarded one year in jail for running a factory that manufactured *kirpans* (one of the religious symbols of the Sikhs): to which another three years were added, on charges of making seditious speeches.

He was sent to jail in distant Dera Gazi Khan (now a district in Pakistan's Punjab) where, in protest against the forced removal of the turbans of Sikh and the 'Gandhi caps' of non-Sikh political prisoners, he discarded all his clothes except his *kachahira* (underpants) – another of the religious symbols of the Sikhs. Despite the extreme weather conditions of the place, he remained bare-backed until he was released after his full term (twice extended for non-obedience of orders) on 4 June, 1927.

Struggle against British Rule

Babaji organised a mammoth demonstration in 1928 when the Simon Commission visited Lahore. Also during 1928-29, he vehemently opposed the Nehru Committee Report until the Congress Party shelved it and took action to secure the Sikhs' concurrence in the framing of constitutional proposals in the future. He was again sent to jail in 1931 but was released after six months. He was re-arrested in 1932 and served another 19 months in prison.

He spoke out in opposition to the Communal Award, which gave a statutory majority to Muslims in the Punjab, and was in and out of jail on several occasions for making speeches that the British government held to be seditious. In 1935, he was, once again, taken into custody for his scathing criticism of the Communal Award.

In 1940, Babaji was again sent to jail for participating in the *satyagraha* movement, but in spite of his old age, Babaji did not stop his activities.

□

13

Badal Gupta

(1912 – 8 December, 1930)

Badal Gupta's real name was Sudhir Gupta. He was an Indian revolutionary who is noted for launching an attack on the Secretariat building – the Writers' Building at Dalhousie Square in Calcutta, along with Benoy Basu and Dinesh Gupta.

Badal Gupta was born in the village, Purba Shimulia (east Shimulia) in the Bikrampur region of Dacca, now in Munshiganj district, Bangladesh. Badal Gupta was also influenced by the revolutionary activities of his two paternal uncles, the late Dharaninath Gupta and Nagendranath Gupta, who were involved in the Alipore Bomb Case and were imprisoned along with Aurobindo Ghosh. Badal Gupta joined the Bengal Volunteers in 1928.

Bengal Volunteers targeted Lt. Colonel N.S. Simpson, the Inspector General of Prisons, who was infamous for oppression of prisoners in jails.The revolutionaries decided not only to murder him, but also to strike a terror in the British official circles by launching an attack on the Secretariat building – the Writers' building at Dalhousie Square in Calcutta.

On 8 December, 1930, Badal along with Dinesh Gupta and Benoy, dressed in European dress, entered the Writers' Building and shot dead Simpson. Police in the building started firing at them in response. What ensued was a brief gunfight between the three young revolutionaries and the police. Some other officers, like Twynam, Prentice and Nelson suffered injuries during the shooting. Soon police overpowered them. However, the three did not wish to be arrested. Badal took potassium cyanide, while Benoy and Dinesh shot themselves with their own revolvers. Badal died on the spot. He was only nineteen-years old when this incident took place.

After Independence, the Dalhousie Square was named B.B.D. Bagh, after the Benoy-Badal-Dinesh trio. In memory of their Writers' Building attack, a plate was engraved on the wall of Writers' Building, first floor. □

14

Baji Rout

(5 October, 1926 – 11 October, 1938)

Baji Rout was the youngest Indian freedom fighter and martyr, having been killed at the age of twelve. He was born on 5 October, 1926. Rout, who was a boat-boy, was shot by the British police when he refused to ferry them across the Brahmani river on the night of 11 October, 1938 at Nilakanthapur Ghat, Bhuban, Dhenkanal district.

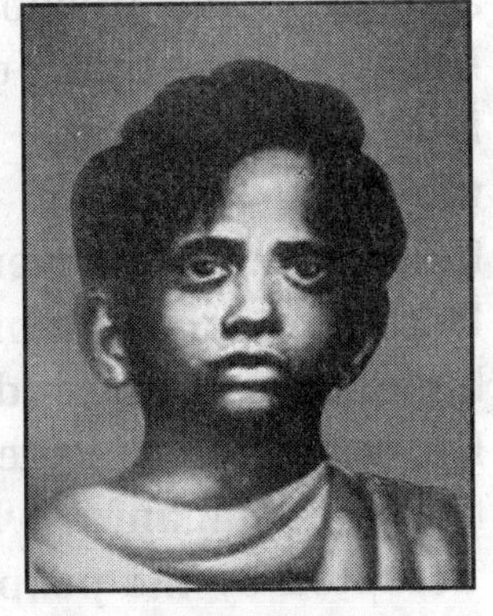

Baji Rout was the youngest son of a boatman on the Brahmani river. As an active member of the Banar Sena of Prajamandal (Party of People), he had volunteered to keep watch by the river at night. The British police force ordered him to ferry them across the river by his boat but he denied. The police force then fired upon Baji Rout along with Laxman Malik, Fagu Sahoo, Hrushi Pradhan and Nata Malik.

□

15

Balgangadhar Tilak

(23 July, 1856 – 1 August, 1920)

Balgangadhar Tilak, born as Keshav Gangadhar Tilak, was an Indian nationalist, teacher and an activist in the freedom struggle. IHe was one-third of the Lal-Bal-Pal triumvirate. Tilak was the first leader of the Indian Independence movement. The British colonial authorities called him 'father of the Indian unrest'. He was also conferred with the title of 'Lokmanya', which means 'accepted by the people (as their leader)'. Mahatma Gandhi called him 'Maker of Modern India'.

Tilak was one of the first and strongest advocates of *swaraj* (self-rule) and a strong radical in Indian consciousness. He is known for his quote in Marathi: "*Swarajya* is my birthright and I shall have it!" He formed a close alliance with many Indian National Congress leaders, including Bipin Chandra Pal, Lala Lajpat Rai, Aurobindo Ghose, V.O. Chidambaram Pillai and Muhammad Ali Jinnah.

Keshav Gangadhar Tilak was born on 23 July, 1856 in a Marathi Hindu Chitpavan Brahmin family at Ratnagiri, the headquarters of the present-day Maharashtra (then Bombay Presidency). His ancestral village was Chikhali. His father, Gangadhar Tilak was a school teacher and a Sanskrit scholar, who died when Tilak was sixteen years of age. In 1871, Tilak was married to Tapibai (*née* Bal) when he was sixteen, a few months before his father's death. Tilak had a long political career, agitating for Indian autonomy from British colonial rule. Before Gandhi, he was the most widely known Indian political leader. Unlike his fellow Maharashtrian contemporary, Gokhale, Tilak was considered a radical nationalist but a social conservative. He was imprisoned on a number of occasions that included a long stint at Mandalay. At one stage in his political life, he was called 'Father of Indian Unrest' by British author Sir Valentine Chirol.

Tilak joined the Indian National Congress in 1890. He opposed its moderate attitude, especially towards the fight for self-government. He was one of the most eminent radicals at the time. In fact, it was the *swadeshi* movement of 1905-1907 that resulted in the split within the Indian National Congress into the Moderates and Extremists.

In late 1896, bubonic plague spread from Bombay to Pune, and by January 1897, it reached epidemic proportions. The British Indian Army was brought in to deal with the emergency and strict measures were employed to curb the plague, including the allowance of forced entry into private houses, examination of the house's occupants, evacuation to hospitals and quarantine camps, removing and destroying personal possessions, and preventing patients from entering or leaving the city. By the end of May, the epidemic was under control. The measures used to curb the pandemic caused widespread resentment among the Indian public. Tilak took up this issue by publishing inflammatory articles in his paper, *Kesari* (*Kesari* was written in Marathi, and *Maratha* was written in English), quoting the Hindu scripture, the *Bhagavad Gita,* to say that no blame could be attached to anyone who killed an oppressor without any thought of reward. Following this, on 22 June, 1897, Commissioner Rand and another British officer, Lt. Ayerst were shot and killed by the Chapekar brothers and their other associates. According to Barbara and Thomas R. Metcalf, Tilak "almost surely concealed the identities of the perpetrators". Tilak was charged with incitement to murder and sentenced to 18 months' imprisonment.

When he emerged from prison in Bombay, he was revered as a martyr and a national hero. He adopted a new slogan coined by his associate Kaka Baptista: "*Swaraj* (self-rule) is my birthright and I shall have it." On 30 April, 1908, two Bengali youths, Prafulla Chaki and Khudiram Bose, threw a bomb on a carriage at Muzaffarpur to kill the Chief Presidency Magistrate Douglas Kingsford of Calcutta fame, but erroneously killed two women travelling in it. While Chaki committed suicide when caught, Bose was hanged. Tilak, in his paper *Kesari*, defended the revolutionaries and called for immediate *swaraj* or self-rule. The government swiftly charged him with sedition. At the conclusion of the trial, a special jury convicted him by 7:2 majority. The judge, Dinshaw D. Davar gave him a six years' jail sentence to be served in Mandalay, Burma and a fine of Rs. 1,000. On being asked by the judge whether he had anything to say, Tilak said: "All that I wish to say is that, in spite of the verdict of the jury, I still maintain that I am innocent. There are higher powers that rule the destinies of men and nations and I think, it may be the will of Providence that the cause I represent may be benefited more by my suffering than by my pen and tongue."

On 28 July, 1956, a portrait of B.G. Tilak was put up in the Central Hall of Parliament House. The portrait of Tilak, painted by Gopal Deuskar, was unveiled by the then Prime Minister of India, Jawaharlal Nehru. □

16

Bankim Chandra Chatterjee

(27 June, 1836 – 8 April, 1894)

Bankim Chandra was an Indian novelist, poet and journalist. He was the composer of *Vande Mataram*, originally in Sanskrit, personifying India as a Mother Goddess and inspiring activists during the Indian Independence movement. Chattopadhyay wrote fourteen novels and many serious, serio-comic, satirical, scientific and critical treatises in Bengali. Chattopadhyay was born in the village of Kanthalpara in the town of North 24 Parganas, Naihati, in an orthodox Bengali Brahmin family as the youngest of three brothers, to Yadav Chandra Chattopadhyaya and Durgadebi. His ancestors hailed from Deshmukho village in Hooghly district. His father, a government official, went on to become the Deputy Collector of Midnapore. One of his brothers, Sanjib Chandra Chattopadhyay was also a novelist and is known for his book, *Palamau*. Bankim Chandra and his elder brother went to Hooghly Collegiate School (then Governmental Zilla School),

where he wrote his first poem. He was educated at the Hooghly Mohsin College and later at Presidency College, Calcutta, graduating with a degree in Arts in 1858. He later attended the University of Calcutta and was one of the two candidates to pass the final exam to become the school's first graduates. He later obtained a degree in Law, in 1869. Following his father's footsteps, Bankim Chandra joined the Subordinate Executive Service. In 1858, he was appointed a Deputy Magistrate (the same type of position held by his father) of Jessore. After merging of the services in 1863, he went on to become the Deputy Magistrate & Deputy Collector, retiring from government service in 1891. His years at work were replete with incidents that brought him into conflict with the colonial government. He was, however, made a Companion of the Most Eminent Order of the Indian Empire (CMEOIE) in 1894. He also received the title of 'Rai Bahadur' in 1891.

Chattopadhyay's earliest publications were in Ishwar Chandra Gupta's weekly newspaper, *Sangbad Prabhaka*. He began his literary career as a writer of verse before turning to fiction. His first attempt was a novel in Bengali, submitted for a declared prize. He did not win and the novelette was never published. His first fiction to appear in print was the English novel *Rajmohan's Wife*. *Durgeshnondini*, his first Bengali romance and the first ever novel in Bengali, was published in 1865.

One of the many novels of Chattopadhyay that are entitled to be termed as historical fiction is *Rajsimha* (1881, rewritten and enlarged 1893). *Anandamath* (The Abbey of Bliss, 1882) is a political novel which depicts a *sannyasi* (Hindu ascetic) army fighting a British force.

The book calls for the rise of Indian nationalism. The novel was also the source of the song *Vande Mataram* (I worship my motherland for she truly is my mother) which, set to music by Rabindranath Tagore, was taken up by many Indian nationalists and is now the national anthem of India. The plot of the novel is loosely set on the *sannyasi* rebellion. He imagined untrained *sannyasi* soldiers fighting and defeating the highly experienced British Army; ultimately, however, he accepted that the British could not be defeated. The novel first appeared in serial form in *Bangadarshan*, the literary magazine that Chattopadhyay founded in 1872. *Vande Mataram* became prominent during the *swadeshi* movement, which was sparked by Lord Curzon's attempt to Partition Bengal into a Hindu-majority West and Muslim-majority East Pakistan. Drawing from the Shakti tradition of Bengali Hindus, Chattopadhyay personified India as a Mother Goddess and this gave the song a Hindu undertone.

□

17

Batukeshwar Dutt

(18 November, 1910 – 20 July, 1965)

Batukeshwar Dutt was an Indian revolutionary and Independence fighter in the early 1900s. He is best known for having exploded a few bombs, along with Bhagat Singh, in the Central Legislative Assembly at New Delhi, on 8 April, 1929. To subdue the rise of revolutionaries, like Bhagat Singh, the British Government decided to implement the Defence of India Act 1915, which gave the police a free hand. Influenced by a French anarchist who had bombed the French Chamber of Deputies, Singh proposed to the HSRA his plan to explode a bomb inside the Central Legislative Assembly, which was agreed. Initially it was decided that Dutt and Sukhdev would plant the bomb, while Singh would travel to the USSR. However, later the plan was changed and Dutt was entrusted with planting it alongside Singh. On 8 April, 1929, Singh and Dutt threw two bombs inside the assembly, rushing in from the Visitor's Gallery. The smoke from the bomb filled the hall and they shouted

slogans of '*Inquilab_Zindabad*' and showered leaflets. The leaflets claimed that the act was done to oppose the Trade Disputes and the Public Safety Bill being presented in the Central Assembly and the death of Lala Lajpat Rai. A few sustained injuries in the explosion but there were no deaths; Singh and Dutt claimed that the act was intentional, so they were arrested as planned.

After his release from prison, Dutt contracted tuberculosis. He nonetheless participated in the Quit India movement of Mahatma Gandhi and was again jailed for four years. He was lodged in Motihari Jail (in Champaran district of Bihar). After India gained Independence, he married Anjali in November 1947. Independent India did not accord him any recognition and he spent his remaining life in poverty, away from political limelight. The later life of the freedom fighter was painful and tragic. On being released from jail due to tuberculosis, he was not valued in Independent India; he grappled with destitution. He was forced into starting a transport business for livelihood. Dutt outlived all his comrades (except Jaydev Kapoor) and died on 20 July, 1965 in the AIIMS Hospital at Delhi, after a long illness. He was cremated in Hussainiwala, near Firozepur in Punjab, where the bodies of his comrades Bhagat Singh, Rajguru and Sukhdev were also cremated years before. He was survived by his only daughter, Bharti Dutt Bagchi, in Patna where his house was situated in the Jakkanpur area. He was one of the writers of the film '*Shaheed*' (1965).

□

18

Benoy Krishna Basu

(11 September, 1908 – 13 December, 1930)

Benoy Krishna Basu was an Indian revolutionary who fought against British rule in India and is known for launching an attack on the Secretariat building; the Writers' Building at Dalhousie Square in Calcutta, along with Badal Gupta and Dinesh Chandra Gupta.

Basu was born on 11 September, 1908, in village Rohitbhog of Munshiganj district, now in Bangladesh. His father Rebatimohan Basu was an engineer.

After passing the Matriculation Examination in Dacca, Benoy enrolled at the Mitford Medical School (now Sir Salimullah Medical College). Under the influence of Hemchandra Ghosh, a revolutionary of Dacca, Benoy joined the Mukti Sangha, a secret society closely connected with the Jugantar Party. He could not complete his medical studies due to his association with revolutionary activities.

Basu and his peer revolutionaries joined the Bengal

Volunteers, a group organised by Subhas Chandra Bose in 1928, on the occasion of the Calcutta session of the Indian National Congress. Soon Benoy started a local unit of the organisation at Dacca and named Bengal Volunteers. Later, the Bengal Volunteers became a more active revolutionary association and prepared a plan for Operation Freedom against police repression in Bengal, especially against the inhuman treatment meted out to political prisoners in different jails. In August 1930, the revolutionary group planned to kill Lowman, the Inspector General of Police who was due to be present in the Medical School Hospital to see an ailing senior police official undergoing treatment. On 29 August, 1930, Benoy casually clad in the traditional Bengali attire, breached the security and fired at close range. Lowman died instantly and Hodson, the Superintendent of Police, was grievously injured. His identity was never a secret. A copy of his photo was taken out of college magazine and pasted all over. A reward of Rs. 10,000/- was announced, but Benoy was far from helping anyone to receive it. He was ultimately caught only to die at the Medical College Hospital in Calcutta, after the Battle of the Verandah. In August, there were torrential rains in East Bengal. One such morning, two Muslim villagers, with tatters covering their bare bodies, were seen wading through knee-deep water. The nearest railway station, Dolaiganj, was their destination. They entered the platform which was swarming with policemen. Benoy's photo was pasted all around.

The train from Dacca to Narayanganj arrived. Every compartment was searched thoroughly. Benoy and his companion got into a third-class compartment which was already over-crowded. When the train reached

Narayanganj, the police searched not only the train but had instructions to search the boats also. A river had to be crossed before one could reach Calcutta. Benoy came to know of it through his own sources. When the train slowed down near a flag station, he began to walk towards the *ghat* to hire a boat to cross the turbulent River Meghna. They changed their dress from Muslim beggars in tatters to one of a *zamindar* with a servant. For a while they had to travel by a steamer. The entire episode was like a scene from a film. The name of his companion was Supati Roy. On reaching the city, they avoided Sealdah, the terminus, and got down at Dum Dum, a small wayside station.

The journey from there to the slum area No. 7, Waliullah Lane in central Calcutta, was somewhat uneventful. A senior activist, Haridas Dutta, arranged shelter for them but a long stay for unknown persons could arouse suspicion. Benoy shifted to a colliery at Katras Garh and from there to a peaceful place in north Calcutta. But he always had the premonition that the police would soon find him out. His fear proved correct when the police chief, Sir Charles Tegart, arrived there with a posse of policemen. By this point, however, Benoy had fled.

The next target was Lt Colonel N.S. Simpson of the Indian Imperial Police and the then Inspector General of Police (Prisons), who was infamous for inflicting the worst form of atrocities on the inmates of the jails. The revolutionaries decided not only to murder him, but also to strike terror in the British official circles by launching an attack on the Secretariat Building – the Writers' Building at Dalhousie Square in Calcutta.

On 8 December, 1930, Benoy along with Dinesh

Gupta and Badal Gupta, dressed in European attire, entered the Writers' Building and shot dead Simpson in his office. Simpson was shot seven times with three bullets to his head. With the police headquarters adjacent to the Secretariat, reinforcements soon arrived and the building was put under lockdown. The revolutionaries managed to evade the responders for some time but were eventually cornered on the second-floor verandah. Thus, *The Statesman* termed this fight between the trio and the police force as 'corridor warfare'. What followed was a short and bloody skirmish as police swarmed into the verandah from both ends. Senior European officers, like McGregor, Twynam, Prentice, Nelson, and Gresham suffered injuries during the shooting.

Soon they were nearly out of ammunition. However, the three did not wish to be arrested. Badal took potassium cyanide, while Benoy and Dinesh shot themselves with their own revolvers.

Photo of injured Benoy Basu, after he attempted to commit suicide with his revolver, inside Writer's Building, Calcutta.

Benoy was taken to the hospital but he died on 13 December, 1930 because he constantly kept injuring himself on the spot where the bullet had hit him.

The martyrdom and self-sacrifice of Benoy, Badal and Dinesh inspired further revolutionary activities in Bengal in particular and India, in general. After Indian Independence, the Dalhousie Square was trnamed B.B.D. Bagh, after the Benoy-Badal-Dinesh trio. In thir memory, a plate was engraved on the wall of Writers' Building, first floor.

□

19

Bhagwati Charan Vohra

(15 November, 1903 – 28 May, 1930)

Bhagwati Charan Vohra was an Indian revolutionary, associated with the Hindustan Socialist Republican Association. He was an ideologue, organiser, orator and a campaigner. Vohra left college to join the non-co-operation movement in 1921 and after the movement was called off, he joined the National College at Lahore, from where he obtained his BA degree. It was here that he was initiated into the revolutionary movement. He, along with Bhagat Singh and Sukhdev, started a study circle on the model of the Russian Socialist Revolution.

Vohra was an avid reader. He played a key role in infusing intellectual ideology in the functioning roots of the organisations he worked with. He was not influenced by caste prejudices but worked for Hindu-Muslim unity as well as the upliftment of the poor by use of socialist principles.

In 1926, when the Naujawan Bharat Sabha

revolutionary organisation was formed by his friend, he was appointed the propaganda secretary of the organisation. On 6 April, 1928, Vohra and Bhagat Singh prepared the manifesto of Naujwan Bharat Sabha and urged the young Indians to have the triple motto – 'service, suffering, sacrifice', as their sole guide to achieve the goal of Independence.

In September 1928, many young revolutionaries met at Ferozshah Kotla grounds in Delhi and reorganised the Hindustan Republican Association into the Hindustan Socialist Republican Association (HSRA), under the leadership of Chandrashekhar Azad. Vohra was appointed propaganda secretary and prepared the HSRA manifesto that was widely distributed at the time of the Lahore session of the Congress. He was also party to murder of J.P. Saunders and the throwing of bombs in the Central Assembly Hall by Singh and Batukeshwar Dutt. Vohra died in Lahore, on 28 May, 1930 while testing a bomb on the banks of River Ravi. The device was required for the proposed rescue of Singh and others undertrials in the Lahore Conspiracy Case but it exploded during the test and he was severely wounded.

He was survived by his wife Durgawati Devi.

□

20

Bhikaiji Rustom Cama

(24 September, 1861 – 13 August, 1936)

Bhikaiji Rustom Cama was one of the prominent figures in the Indian Independence movement. Bhikaiji Cama was born in Bombay (now Mumbai) in a large, well-off Parsee family. Her parents, Sorabji Framji Patel and Jaijibai Sorabji Patel, were well known in the city, where her father Sorabji, a lawyer by training and a merchant by profession, was an influential member of the Parsee community.

She was invited to hoist the flag over the Parliament in Germany.

In October 1896, the Bombay Presidency was hit first by famine and shortly thereafter by bubonic plague. Bhikhaiji joined one of the many teams working out of Grant Medical College (which would subsequently become Haffkine's Plague Vaccine Research Centre), in an effort to provide care for the afflicted and (later) to inoculate the healthy. Cama subsequently contracted the plague herself, but managed to survive. As she was severely weakened, she was sent to Britain for medical care in 1902.

She was preparing to return to India in 1908, when she came in contact with Shyamji Krishna Varma, who was well known among London's Indian community for fiery nationalist speeches he gave at Hyde Park. Through him, she met Dadabhai Naoroji, then president of the British Committee of the Indian National Congress, and for whom she came to work as private secretary. Toge ther with Naoroji and Singh Rewabhai Rana, Cama supported the founding of Varma's Indian Home Rule Society in February 1905. In London, she was told that her return to India would be prevented unless she signed a statement promising not to participate in nationalist activities.

On 22 August, 1907, Cama attended the second Socialist Congress at Stuttgart, Germany, where she described the devastating effects of a famine that had struck the Indian sub-continent. In her appeal for human rights, equality and for autonomy from Great Britain, she unfurled what she called the 'Flag of Indian Independence'. It has been speculated that this moment may have been an inspiration for African American writer and intellectual W.E.B. Du Bois who wrote his 1928 novel, *Dark Princess*. Cama's flag, a modification of the Calcutta flag, was co-designed by Cama and Vinayak Damodar Savarkar, and would later serve as one of the templates from which the current national flag of India was created.

In 1909, following Madan Lal Dhingra's assassination of William Hutt Curzon Wyllie, an aide to the Secretary of State for India, Scotland Yard arrested several key activists living in Great Britain, among whom was Vinayak Damodar Savarkar. In 1910, Savarkar was ordered to return to India for trial. When the ship, Savarkar was being transported on, docked in Marseilles harbour, he squeezed out through a porthole window and jumped into the sea. Reaching ashore, he expected to find Cama and others who had been told to expect him (who got there late), but ran into the local constabulary instead. Unable to communicate his predicament to the French authorities without Cama's help, he was returned to British custody. The British Government requested for Cama's extradition, but the French Government refused to cooperate. In return, the British Government seized Cama's inheritance. Influenced by Christabel Pankhurst and the Suffragette movement, Bhikhaiji Cama was vehement in her support of gender equality. Speaking at Cairo, Egypt in 1910, she asked, "I see here the representatives of only half the population of Egypt. May I ask where is the other half? Sons of Egypt, where are the daughters of Egypt? Where are your mothers and sisters? Your wives and daughters?" Cama's stance with respect to the vote for women was, however, secondary to her position on Indian Independence. In 1920, upon meeting Herabai and Mithan Tata, two Parsee women who were outspoken on the issue of the right to vote, Cama is said to have sadly shaken her head and observed: "'Work for Indian's freedom and Independence. When India is independent, women will not only have the right to vote, but all other rights."

☐

21

Bhogeswari Phukanani

(1885 – 21 September, 1942)

Bhogeswari Phukanani was an activist in the Indian Independence movement during the British Raj and played a role in the freedom struggle. Phukanani was born in Nagaon district, Assam, in 1885. She was married to Bhogeswar Phukan and the couple had two daughters and six sons. Even though she was a mother of eight and a housewife, Phukanani played an important role in the Quit India movement.

Phukanani was active in Berhampur, Babajia and Barpujia areas of Nagaon district of Assam and helped set up offices for the Indian National Congress. In 1930, Phukanani took part in a non-violent march as an act of civil disobedience against the British authorities and was arrested for picketing.

During the Indian Independence movement, Phukanani would often take part in non-violent protest marches against the British rule. In 1942, the Berhampur Indian National Congress office was seized by the British authorities and closed. Phukanani and her sons took part in that protest march and a successful attempt was made to reopen the Congress office. A celebration of the office's reopening was held on 18 September, 1942, or perhaps two days later. The British sent a large force to lock the Congress office, and possibly to have it destroyed.

There are at least two accounts of the events surrounding Phukanani's death. According to one, Phukanani and someone named Ratnamala were leading a large group of people, including many from the surrounding villages and were carrying the Indian national flag and shouting '*Vande Mataram*' and freedom slogans. The police resisted the group with force and in the ensuing scuffle, a British Army captain named Finish grabbed the national flag from Ratnamala, who fell to the ground. Seeing this as an insult to the Indian national flag, Phukanani struck the captain with the pole of a flag that she herself was carrying. According to another, Phukanani was not present when the British arrived and demanded that the crowd demolish the Congress office, but when she came, she noticed a British official named Finch pointing a gun at her son and other protesters. Rushing forward, she struck the official with a flag pole. In these accounts, the man she struck – Finch or Finish – then shot her. Phukanani succumbed to the gunshot wound either that day (20 September, 1942), or three days later an 18 September, 1942 due to injury.

After India gained Independence in 1947, a hospital and an indoor stadium were named after her. The hospital was established in 1854 at Nagaon, Assam, by an American Baptist missionary Miles Bronsonis and was later renamed Bhogeswari Phukanani Civil Hospital. The indoor stadium named after her is situated at Gauhati in Assam.

□

22

Birsa Munda

(15 November, 1875 – 9 June, 1900)

Birsa Munda was an Indian tribal freedom fighter, religious leader and folk-hero who belonged to the Munda tribe. He spearheaded a tribal religious millenarian movement that arose in the Bengal Presidency (now Jharkhand) in the late 19th century, during the British Raj, thereby making him an important figure in the history of the Indian Independence movement.The revolt mainly concentrated in the Munda belt of Khunti, Tamar, Sarwada and Bandgaon.

His portrait hangs in the Indian Parliament Museum. He is the only tribal leader to have been so honoured.

Birsa Munda was born on 15 November, 1875, at Ulihatu in Lohardaga district of Bengal Presidency (now in Khunti district of Jharkhand) on a Thursday (some sources claim he was born on 18 July, 1872 and not in 1875) and hence named after that day, according to the then prevalent Munda custom. The folk-songs reflect popular confusion and refer to Ulihatu or Chalkad as his birthplace. Ulihatu was the birthplace of Sugana Munda, father of Birsa. The claim of Ulihatu rests on Birsa's elder brother Komta Munda living in the village, where his house still exists, albeit in a dilapidated condition.

Birsa's father, mother Karmi Munda and younger brother Pasna Munda left Ulihatu and proceeded to Kurumbda, near Birbanki, in search of employment as labourers (*sajhedari*) or crop-sharers (*ryots*). At Kurumbda, Birsa's elder brother Komta and his sister Daskir were born. From there, the family moved to Bamba where Birsa's elder sister Champa was born.

Birsa's early years were spent with his parents at Chalkad. His early life could not have been very different from that of an average Munda child. Folklore refers to his rolling and playing in sand and dust with his friends and his growing up strong and handsome in looks. He grazed sheep in the forest of Bohonda. When he grew up, he shared an interest in playing the flute, in which he became an expert. He went around with the *tuila*, the one-stringed instrument made from the pumpkin, in the hand and the flute strung to his waist. Exciting moments of his childhood were spent on the *akhara* (the village wrestling ground). However, one of his ideal contemporaries and who went out with him heard him speak of strange things. Driven by poverty, Birsa was taken to Ayubhatu, his maternal uncle's village. Komta Munda, his eldest brother, who was ten years of age, went to Kundi Bartoli, entered the service of a Munda, married and lived there for eight years, and then joined his father and younger brother at Chalkad. At Ayubhatu, Birsa lived for two years. He went to school at Salga, run by one Jaipal Nag. He accompanied his mother's younger sister Joni, who was fond of him, when she was married to Khatanga, to her new home. He came in contact with a Christian missionary who visited a few families in the village which had been converted to Christianity.

As he was sharp in studies, Jaipal Nag recommended him to join the German Mission School and Birsa converted to Christianity. He was renamed as Birsa David, which later became Birsa Daud. After studying for few years, he left the German Mission School. Birsa's long stay at Chaibasa, from 1886 to 1890, constituted a formative period of his life. This period was marked by the German and Roman Catholic Christian agitation. In light of the freedom struggle, Sugana Munda withdrew his son from the school. Soon after leaving Chaibasa in 1890, Birsa and his family gave up their membership of the German Mission and ceased to be Christian, reverting back to his original traditional tribal religious system.

He left Gorbera in the wake of the mounting Sardar agitation. He participated in the agitation stemming from popular disaffection at the restrictions imposed upon the traditional rights of the Mundas in the protected forest, under the leadership of Gidiun of Piring in the Porhat area. During 1893-94, all waste lands in villages, the ownership of which was vested in the government, were constituted into protected forests under the Indian Forest Act VII of 1882. In west Singhbhum, as in Lohardaga, the forest settlement operations were launched and measures were taken to determine the rights of the forest-dwelling communities. Villages in forests, were marked off in blocks of convenient size and consisted of village sites and cultivable and wastelands sufficient for the needs of the villages. In 1894, when

Birsa had grown up into a strong young man, shrewd and intelligent, he undertook the work of repairing the Dombari tank at Gerbera as it was damaged by rains.

While on a sojourn in the neighbourhood village Sankara, in west Singhbhum district, he found a suitable companion, presented her parents with jewels and explained his idea of marriage. Later, on his return from jail, he did not find her faithful to him and left her. Another woman who served him at Chalkad was the sister of Mathias Munda. On his release from prison, the daughter of Mathura Munda of Koensar, who was kept by Kali Munda and the wife of Jaga Munda of Jiuri, insisted on becoming wives of Birsa. He rebuked them and referred the wife of Jaga Munda to her husband. Another rather well-known woman who stayed with Birsa was Sali of Burudih.

Tribal Movement

Birsa Munda's slogan threatening the British Raj– '*Abua raj ete jana, maharani raj tundu jana*' is still remembered in areas of Jharkhand, Orissa, Bihar, West Bengal, and Madhya Pradesh. The British colonial system intensified the transformation of the tribal agrarian system into a feudal state. As the tribals, with their primitive technology could not generate a surplus, the non-tribal peasantry was invited by the chiefs in Chhotanagpur to settle on and cultivate the land. This led to the alienation of the lands held by the tribals. The new class of *thikadars* was of a more rapacious kind and eager to make the most of their possessions. In 1856, *jagirs* stood at about 600, and they held from a village to 150 villages. But by 1874, the authority of the old

Munda or Oraon chiefs was almost entirely annulled by that of the farmers introduced by the landlords. In some villages, they completely lost their proprietary rights and were reduced to the position of farm labourers.

To the twin challenges of agrarian breakdown and culture change, Birsa along with the Munda responded through a series of revolts and uprisings under his leadership. In 1895, in Chalkad village of Tamar, Birsa Munda renounced Christianity, asked his fellow tribesmen to worship only one God and give up the worship of *bongas*. He declared himself a prophet who had come to recover the lost kingdom of his people. He said that the reign of Queen Victoria was over and the Munda Raj had begun. He gave orders to the *ryots* (tenant farmers) to pay no rents. The Mundas called him 'Dharati Aaba', 'the father of earth'.

Due to a rumour that those who didn't follow Birsa would be massacred, Birsa was arrested on 24 August, 1895 and sentenced to two-year imprisonment. On 28 January, 1898, after being released from jail, he went with his followers to Chutia to collect the record and to re-establish racial links with the temple. He said that the temple belonged to the Kols. The Christian missionaries wanted to arrest Birsa and his followers, who were threatening their ability to make converts. Birsa went underground for two years but attended a series of secret meetings. During this period he visited the Jagannath temple.

It is said that around 7,000 men and women assembled around Christmas of 1899, to herald the *ulgulaan* (revolution) which soon spread to Khunti, Tamar, Basia and Ranchi. The Anglican Mission at Murhu and the Roman Catholic Mission at Sarwada were the main targets. The Birsaits openly declared that the real enemies were the British and not Christian Mundas and called for a decisive war against the British. For two years, they attacked places loyal to the British.

On 5 January, 1900, Birsa's followers killed two constables at Etkedih. On January 7, they attacked Khunti police station, killed a constable and razed the houses of local shopkeepers. The Commissioner A. Fobes and Deputy Commissioner H.C. Streattfield rushed to Khunti with an army of 150 to crush the rebellion. The British administration set a reward of Rs. 500 for capture of Birsa. The British forces attacked Munda guerrillas at Dumbari Hill, indiscriminately firing on and killing hundreds of people. Birsa escaped to the hills of Singhbhum. He was arrested at Jamkopai forest in Chakradharpur on 3 February, 1900. According to Deputy Commissioner of Ranchi, vide a letter, 460 tribals were made accused in 15 different criminal cases, out of which 63 were convicted. One was sentenced to death, 39 to transportation for life and 23 to imprisonment for terms up to fourteen years. There were six deaths, including that of Birsa Munda in prison during the trials. Birsa Munda died in jail on 9 June, 1900. After his death, the movement faded out. In 1908, the colonial government introduced the Chhotanagpur Tenancy Act (CNT), which prohibits the transfer of tribal land to non-tribals.

□

23

Chakravarti Rajagopalachari

(9 December, 1878 – 25 December, 1972)

Popularly known as Rajaji or C.R. and also as Mootharignar Rajaji. (Rajaji, the scholar emeritus), was an Indian statesman, writer, lawyer and activist in the struggle for Independence. Rajagopalachari was the last Governor-General of India when the country became a republic in 1950. He was also the first India-born Governor-General as all the previous holders of the post were British nationals. He also served as leader of the Indian National Congress, premier of Madras Presidency, Governor of West Bengal, Minister for Home Affairs of the Indian Union and Chief Minister of Madras state. Rajagopalachari founded the Swatantra Party and was one of the first recipients of India's highest civilian award, the Bharat Ratna. He vehemently opposed the use of nuclear weapons and was a proponent of world peace and disarmament. During his lifetime, he also acquired the nickname 'Mango of Salem'.

Rajagopalachari was born in the Thorapalli village

of Hosur *taluka* of Krishnagiri district in Tamil Nadu and was educated at Central College, Bangalore and at the Presidency College, Madras. In the 1900s, he started his legal practice at the Salem court. On entering politics, he became a member and later chairperson of the Salem municipality. One of Mahatma Gandhi's earliest political lieutenants, he joined the Indian National Congress and participated in agitations against the Rowlatt Act, joining the non-co-operation movement, the Vaikom *satyagraha* and the Civil Disobedience movement. In 1930, Rajagopalachari risked imprisonment when he led the Vedaranyam salt *aatyagraha* in response to the Dandi March. In 1937, Rajagopalachari was elected Prime Minister of the Madras Presidency and served until 1940, when he resigned due to Britain's declaration of war on Germany. He later advocated co-operation over Britain's war effort and opposed the Quit India movement. He favoured talks with both Muhammad Ali Jinnah and the Muslim League and proposed what later came to be known as the C.R. formula. In 1946, Rajagopalachari was appointed Minister of Industry, Supply, Education and Finance in the Interim Government of India, and then as the Governor of West Bengal, from 1947 to 1948, Governor-General of India from 1948 to 1950, Union Home Minister from 1951 to 1952 and as Chief Minister of Madras state from 1952 to 1954. In 1959, he resigned from the Indian National Congress and founded the Swatantra Party, which fought against the Congress in the 1962, 1967 and 1971 elections. Rajagopalachari was instrumental in setting up a united anti-Congress front in Madras state under C.N. Annadurai, who swept the 1967 elections. C.R. died on 25 December, 1972 at the age of 94.

Rajagopalachari's interest in public affairs and politics began when he commenced his legal practice at Salem in 1900. At the age of 28, he joined the Indian National Congress and participated as a delegate in the 1906 Calcutta session. Inspired by the Indian Independence activist Bal Gangadhar Tilak, he became a member of the Salem municipality in 1911. In 1917, he was elected chairman of the municipality and served from 1917 to 1919, during which time he was responsible for the election of the first Dalit member of the Salem municipality. In 1917, he defended Indian Independence activist P. Varadarajulu Naidu against charges of sedition and two years later, participated in the agitations against the Rowlatt Act. Rajagopalachari was a close friend of the founder of *swadeshi* Steam Navigation Company V.O. Chidambaram Pillai as well as greatly admired by Indian Independence activists, Annie Besant and C. Vijayaraghavachariar.

After Mahatma Gandhi joined the Indian Independence movement in 1919, Rajagopalachari became one of his followers. He participated in the non-co-operation movement and gave up his law practice. In 1921, he was elected to the Congress Working Committee and served as the General Secretary of the party before making his first major breakthrough as a leader during the 1922 Indian National Congress session at Gaya, where he strongly opposed collaboration with the colonial administration and participation in the diarchial legislatures established under the Government of India Act 1919. While Gandhi was in prison, Rajagopalachari led the group of 'No Changers' and these individuals were against contesting elections for the Imperial Legislative

Council and other Provincial Legislative Councils, in opposition to the 'Pro Changers' who advocated Council entry. When the motion was put to the vote, the 'No Changers' won by 1,748 to 890 votes, resulting in the resignation of important Congress leaders, including Pandit Motilal Nehru and C.R. Das, the president of the Indian National Congress. When the Indian National Congress split in 1923, Rajagopalachari was a member of the Civil Disobedience Enquiry Committee. He was also involved in the Vaikom *satyagraha* movement against Untouchability during 1924-25. In a public speech on 27 May, 1924, he reassured the anxious upper caste Hindus in Vaikom, "Mahatmaji does not want the caste system abolished but holds that untouchability should be abolished...Mahatmaji does not want you to dine with the Thiyyas or the Pulayas; what he wants is that we must be prepared to go near or touch other human beings as you go near a cow or a horse."

In the early 1930s, Rajagopalachari emerged as one of the major leaders of the Tamil Nadu Congress. When Gandhi organised the Dandi march in 1930, Rajagopalachari broke the salt law at Vedaranyam, near Nagapattinam, along with Indian Independence activist Sardar Vedaratnam. Rajagopalachari was sentenced to six-months of rigorous imprisonment and was sent to the Trichinopoly Central Prison. He was subsequently elected president of the Tamil Nadu Congress Committee. Following the enactment of the Government of India Act in 1935, Rajagopalachari was instrumental in persuading the Indian National Congress to participate in the 1937 General Elections.

Second World War

Some months after the outbreak of the Second World War, Rajagopalachari resigned as premier along with other members of his cabinet in protest at the declaration of war by the Viceroy of India. Rajagopalachari was arrested in December 1940, in accordance with the Defence of India rules and sentenced to one year in prison. However, subsequently, Rajagopalachari differed in opposition to the British war effort. He also opposed the 'Quit India' movement and instead advocated dialogue with the British. He reasoned that passivity and neutrality would be harmful to India's interests at a time when the country was threatened with invasion. He also advocated dialogue with the Muslim League, which was demanding the Partition of India. He subsequently resigned from the party and the assembly following differences over resolutions passed by the Madras Congress Legislative Party and disagreements with the leader of the Madras provincial Congress, K. Kamaraj.

Following the end of the war in 1945, elections followed in the Madras Presidency in 1946. During the last years of the war, Kamaraj was requested by Nehru, Sardar Vallabhbhai Patel and Maulana Abul Kalam Azad to make Rajagopalachari the premier of Madras Presidency. Kamaraj, president of the Tamil Nadu Congress Committee, was forced to appoint Tanguturi Prakasam as Chief Ministerial candidate, by the elected members, to prevent Rajagopalachari from winning. However, Rajagopalachari did not contest the elections and Prakasam was elected.

Rajagopalachari was instrumental in initiating negotiations between Gandhi and Jinnah. In 1944, he proposed a solution for the Indian constitutional tangle. In the same year, he proposed an 'absolute majority' threshold of 55 per cent when deciding whether a district should become part of India or Pakistan, triggering a huge controversy among nationalists.

From 1946 to 1947, Rajagopalachari served as the Minister for Industry, Supply, Education, and Finance in the Interim Government headed by Jawaharlal Nehru.

□

24

Chempakaraman Pillai

(15 September, 1891 – 26 May, 1934)

Chempakaraman Pillai was an India-born political activist and revolutionary. Born at Trivandrum, Kerala, to Tamil parents, he left for Europe as a youth to spend the rest of his active life as an Indian nationalist and revolutionary. Although his life was mired in controversies, including a squabble with Adolf Hitler, information on his life in Europe was sketchy in the immediate years following his death. More information has come out in recent years.

Chempakaraman Pillai is credited with the coining of the salutation and slogan '*Jai Hind*' in the pre-Independence days of India. The slogan is still widely used in India.

The Indian Independence Committee ultimately became involved in the so-called Hindu-German conspiracy along with the Ghadar Party in the United States. The German Foreign Office, under Kaiser Wilhelm II, funded the Committee's anti-British activities.

Chempakaraman and A. Raman Pillai, both from Travancore and both students at German universities, worked together on the Committee. Pillai later allied with the Indian National Army chief, Subhas Chandra Bose.

Many of Pillai's letters to A. Raman Pillai, then a student in the University of Göttingen, were kept by Raman Pillai's son Rosscote Krishna Pillai. The letters reveal some aspects of Pillai's life in Germany between 1914 and 1920, as does one of July 1914, calling upon Indian soldiers in the British Indian Army to rise in revolt and fight against the British.

After the end of World War I and Germany's defeat, Pillai stayed in Germany, working as a technician in a factory at Berlin; when Netaji Subhas Chandra Bose visited Vienna, Pillai met him and explained his plan of action

Pillai was the Foreign Minister of the Provisional Government of India set up in Kabul, Afghanistan on 1 December, 1915, with Raja Mahendra Pratap as president and Maulana Barkatullah as prime minister. However, the defeat of the Germans in the war shattered the hopes of the revolutionaries and the British forced them out of Afghanistan in 1919.

During this time, the Germans were helping the Indian revolutionaries for their own benefits. Though the Indians made it clear to the Germans that they were equal partners in their fight against the common enemy, the Germans wanted to use the revolutionaries' propaganda work and military intelligence for their own purpose. In 1907, Pillai coined the term '*Jai Hind*', which was adopted as a slogan of the Indian National Army in the 1940s at the suggestion of Abid Hasan. After India's

Independence, it emerged as a national slogan.

In 1931, Pillai married Lakshmi Bai of Manipur, whom he had met in Berlin. Unfortunately they had a short life together, as Pillai soon fell ill. There were symptoms of slow poisoning and he went to Italy for treatment. He died in Berlin on 28 May, 1934. Lakshmi Bai brought Pillai's ashes to India, in 1935, where they were later ceremonially immersed at Kanyakumari with full state honours. It was Pillai's final wish that his ashes be sprinkled in Nanjilnadu (Kanyakumari), his family's native place.

□

25

Chhotu Ram

(24 November, 1881 – 9 January, 1945)

Chhotu Ram was a prominent politician in British India's Punjab province, an ideologue of the pre-Independent India and who belonged to the Jat community and championed the interest of oppressed communities of the Indian sub-continent. For this feat, he was knighted in 1937. On the political front, he was a co-founder of the National Unionist Party which ruled the united Punjab province in pre-Independent India and kept Congress and Muslim League at bay.

Chhotu Ram was born as Ram Richpal in a Jat family of the village of Garhi Sampla, Rohtak district, Punjab province. His parents were Chaudhary Sukhiram Singh Ohlian and Sarla Devi. He acquired the nickname Chhotu Ram, as he was the youngest of his brothers

Chhotu Ram joined primary school in January 1891, passing out four years later. When he was around eleven years of age, he married Giano Devi. He studied for his middle school examination at Jhajjar, 12 miles from his village. He then enrolled in the Christian Mission School at Delhi. He passed his intermediate examination in 1903 and proceeded to St. Stephen's College, Delhi from where he graduated in 1905 with a distinction in Sanskrit. He gained his LLB from Agra College in 1910 and began his practice as an advocate in 1912. He started the Anglo-Sanskrit School on 26 March, 1913 in Rohtak. He joined Indian National Congress in 1916. Chhotu Ram worked as the president of the Rohtak District Congress Committee from 1916 to 1920. A part of his education were funded by the prominent Jat philanthropist, Seth Chhaju Ram. After 1920, Ram tried to create a non-sectarian peasant group consciousness. He formed the Unionist Party (Zamindara League) in 1923, which was a cross-communal alliance of Hindu, Sikh, and Muslim agriculturists. He soon aligned with such Muslim leaders, as Fazli Husain.

The Unionist Party won elections in 1935 to form the provincial government in the capital at Lahore. As Revenue Minister, he brought in changes in Law to stop the practice of usury (charging interest on interest). Among the supporters of the party at this point were such prominent urban Muslims, as Abdul Qadir.

Ram initially approved the Bhakra Dam scheme. [citation needed] He got an agreement signed with the Maharaja of Bilaspur, in whose territory the waters of River Sutlej were to be impounded and the Punjab government signed only a few weeks before he died on 9 January, 1945. He studied the *Bhagavad Gita* and was very much influenced by its philosophy. There are many instances which represent his value for education and compassion for the poor. A substantial portion of his salary as minister was set aside for scholarships and stipends for the economically poor but bright students.

The enactment of two agrarian laws was primarily due to his contribution. These were the Punjab Relief Indebtedness Act of 1934 and the Punjab Debtor's Protection Act of 1936, which emancipated the peasants from the clutches of moneylenders and restored the right of land to the tiller.

Ram died at Lahore on 9 January, 1945. His body was carried back to his home in Rohtak city, where it was cremated at the Jat Heroes Memorial Anglo-Sanskrit Senior Secondary School in the presence of thousands of people.

Chhotu Ram was awarded the title of 'Rao Bahadur'. [citation needed] He was knighted in 1937 and was popularly known as Deen Bandhu (in Urdu as Rahbar-e-Azam, which translates as messiah of the poor).

All Punjabis recognised that Chotu Ram's demise possessed profound political consequences. Jat farmers flocked to Rohtak to pay respects at his demise. His legacy has been evoked by the formation of a new party, the National Unionist Zamindara Party by *guar* farmers of Rajasthan in 2013.

Ram's place of residence in Rohtak was known as PremNivas and Nili Kothi. The *chowk* (road square) nearest to his house is now known as Chhotu Ram Chowk and a *dharmshala* exists at the same place, in his name. A *samadhi* (tomb) was created in his memory at the school campus where he was cremated and there people pay homage on his birthday every year.

Chhotu Ram State College of Engineering College

in Murthal (Sonepat district), Haryana, is named after him (the name of the college has since been changed to Deenbandhu Chhotu Ram University of Science and Technology, abbreviated as DCRUST, after it got the university status in 2006).

Sir Chhotu Ram College of Education, Kurukshetra is named after him. Further, Sir Chhotu Ram Institute of Engineering & Technology at Meerut is also named after him. The Indian Government issued a commemorative stamp on 9 January, 1995.

The Jat-Anglo Sanskrit School was started by him on 26 March, 1913 at Rohtak. A Bachelor of Education College at the same campus is also named after him. Ch. Birender Singh, Sir Chhotu Ram's daughter's son got a 64-feet high statue by Ch. Chhotu Ram Trust, Rohtak. It is the highest in Haryana, at his birth site, Garhi Sampla. This statue was unveiled by Prime Minister Narendra Modi on 9 October, 2019.

□

26

Daulat Mal Bhandari

(16 December, 1907 – 10 January, 2004)

Daulat Mal Bhandari was Chief Justice of Rajasthan High Court in India, a member of the first Lok Sabha and a freedom fighter. Bhandari took active part in the freedom struggle. In 1942, he formed the Azad Morcha in Jaipur and staged *satyagraha*. He was imprisoned for nine months. He also organised the Praja Mandal in Jaipur state. During the Partition of India, he contributed in the rehabilitation of refugees from Sindh and western Punjab.

He served as the Development and Agriculture Minister of Jaipur state in 1947 on being elected to the state's Legislative Assembly. Bhandari was a member of the Lok Sabha from 1952 to 1955, representing the Jaipur parliamentary constituency of Rajasthan. Bhandari was a senior advocate on the rolls of the Bar Council of India. He was appointed a judge of the Rajasthan High Court in 1955 and he rose to become the Chief Justice in 1968.

He also served as Chairman of the Revenue Law Commission constituted by the Government of Rajasthan and was a member of the Krishna-Godavari Water Dispute Tribunal constituted by the Government of India. He was a founder member of the Indian Law

Institute in New Delhi. He also served as the Chairman of the Governing Body of the Lal Bahadur Shastri College, Jaipur. He had six sons. Daulat Mal Bhandari died on 10 January, 2004 at Jaipur at the age of 97.

□

27

Dharam Singh Hayatpur

(1884 – 27 February, 1926)

Dharam Singh Hayatpur was a prominent member of the Sikh political and religious group – the Babbar Akali Movement in India. In 1926, a British Imperial Sessions Court sentenced him to life imprisonment for his activities, but this sentence was increased on appeal by the High Court and he was hanged. Dharam Singh Hayatpur and five other men's struggle influenced Bhagat Singh in writing his article, 'Blood Sprinkled on the Day of Holi Babbar Akalis on the Crucifix', which shows admiration for the men and highlights their cause.

□

28

Dinesh Chandra Gupta

(6 December, 1911 – 7 July, 1931)

Dinesh Chandra was an Indian revolutionary who fought against British rule in India and was noted for launching an attack on the Secretariat building – the Writers' Building at Dalhousie Square in Calcutta, along with Badal Gupta and Benoy Basu.

Legendary Rabindra Sangeet exponent and trainer Maya Sen (maiden name, Gupta) was his niece. Even he suggested to his sister-in-law Ashalata Gupta to let Maya learn Rabindra Sangeet. His nephew and Maya's brother Dr. Tapan Gupta was a famous doctor and established 'the Tagoreans' in London. Mr. Gupta's daughter is an MBE, while Tanika Gupta is a well- known playwright and regularly works for BBC and the stage in England.

The association targeted Lt. Colonel N.S. Simpson, the Inspector General of Prisons, who was infamous for brutal oppression of the prisoners in the jails. [citation needed] The revolutionaries decided not only to murder him, but also to strike a terror in the British official circles by launching an attack on the Secretariat building – the Writers' Building at Dalhousie Square in Calcutta.

On 8 December, 1930, Dinesh, along with Benoy Basu and Badal Gupta, dressed in European costumes, entered the Writers' Building and shot dead Simpson. Nearby police started firing at them in response. What ensued was a brief gunfight between the three young revolutionaries and the police. Some other officers, like Twynam, Prentice and Nelson suffered injuries during the shooting.

Soon the police overpowered them. However, the three did not wish to be arrested. Badal Gupta took potassium cyanide, while Benoy and Dinesh shot themselves with their own revolvers. Benoy was taken to the hospital where he died on 13 December, 1930. However, Dinesh survived the near-fatal injury. He was convicted and sentenced to death.

While in Alipore Jail, he wrote letters to his sister and these were later compiled into a book titled, *Ami Shubhash Bolchhi*. He was hanged on 7 July, 1931 at Alipore Jail. Soon after that, Kanailal Bhattacharjee took revenge for the hanging by killing Mr. Galik (the judge of the Dinesh Gupta case) on 27 July, 1931.

□

29

Durgavati Devi

(17 October, 1907 – 15 October, 1999)

Durgavati Devi, popularly known as 'Durga Bhabhi' was an Indian revolutionary and a freedom fighter. She was one of the few women revolutionaries who actively participated in armed revolution against the ruling British Raj. She is best known for having accompanied Bhagat Singh on the train journey in which he made his escape in disguise after the Saunders killing Since she was the wife of Hindustan Socialist Republican Association (HSRA), member Bhagwati Charan Vohra. other members of HSRA referred to her as *Bhabhi* (elder brother's wife) and became popular as "Durga Bhabhi" in Indian revolutionary circles.

After Bhagat Singh surrendered himself for the 1929 Assembly bomb-throwing incident, Durgawati Devi attempted to assassinate Lord Hailey, who escaped, but many of his associates died. She was caught by the police and imprisoned for three years. She had also sold her ornaments worth Rs.3,000 to rescue Bhagat Singh and his comrades under trial.

Devi, along with her husband, helped Vimal Prasad Jain, an HSRA member, in running a bomb factory named 'Himalayan Toilets' (a smokescreen to hide the agenda of making bombs) at Qutub Road, Delhi. In this factory, they handled picric acid, nitroglycerine and fulminate of mercury.

Two days after killing Saunders, on 19 December, 1928, Sukhdev called on Devi to seek her help, which she agreed to do. They decided to catch the train departing from Lahore for Bathinda *en route* to Howrah (Calcutta), early the next morning. She posed as the wife of Bhagat Singh and put her son Sachin in his lap while Rajguru carried their luggage behaving as their servant. To avoid recognition, Singh had shaved off his beard and cut his hair short the previous day and was dressed in Western attire. In fact, when Bhagat Singh and Sukhdev came to her house on the night of 19 December, 1928, Sukhdev introduced Bhagat Singh as a new friend. Devi could not recognise Bhagat Singh at all. Then Sukhdev told Devi the truth and said that if Devi could not recognise Bhagat Singh in his changed clean-shaved appearance despite knowing him well, surely the police would not recognise him as they would be looking for a bearded Sikh.

They left the house early the next morning. At the station, Bhagat Singh, with his concealed identity, bought three tickets for Cawnpore (Kanpur) – two first-class tickets for Devi and himself and a third class one for Rajguru. Both men had loaded revolvers with them to deal with any unanticipated incident. They avoided raising the suspicions of the police and boarded the train. Breaking the journey at Kanpur, they boarded a train for Lucknow since the CID at Howrah Railway Station usually scrutinised passengers on the direct train from Lahore. At Lucknow, Rajguru left separately for Benares while Bhagat Singh, Devi and the infant went to Howrah. Devi returned to Lahore a few days later with her infant child.

Unlike other freedom fighters, after Indian Independence, Durga started living as a common citizen in quiet anonymity and exclusion at Ghaziabad. She later opened a school for poor children in Lecknow. Durgawati Devi died at Ghaziabad on 15 October, 1999 at the age of 92.

□

30

Garimella Satyanarayana

(14 July, 1893 – 18 December, 1952)

Garimella Satyanarayana was a poet and freedom fighter from Andhra Pradesh. He influenced and mobilised the Andhra people against the British Raj with his patriotic songs and writings, for which he was jailed several times by the British administration.

Garimella Satyanarayana was born in a poor family of Gonepadu village, near Priya Agraharam, in Narasannapeta *taluka* of Srikakulam district, in 1893. His parents were Venkatanarasimham and Suramma.

He was helped to study by a kind lawyer, called Kannepalli Narasimha Rao and thus could finish graduation (B.A.). He worked as a clerk in the Collector's office of Ganjam district and as a teacher at a high school in Vijayanagaram. He gave up his studies on the call of Mahatma Gandhi to participate in non-co-operation movement. During this time, he wrote his famous song, '*Maakoddee Telladoratanamu*' for which he was jailed in 1922, for one year. After his release from jail, he continued his participation in the movement by singing songs in villages. For this he was sentenced to two-and-a-half years of rigorous imprisonment. His entire family (wife, father and grandfather) died when he was in jail. He also ran a restaurant called Kalpaka Vilaas.

He died in a destitute condition on 18 December, 1952 after spending several years in poverty.

□

31

George Joseph

(5 June, 1887 – 5 March, 1938)

George Joseph was a lawyer and Indian Independence activist. One of the earliest and among the most prominent Syrian Christians from Kerala to join the freedom struggle, Joseph's working life began in Madurai and he is remembered for his role in the home rule agitation and the Vaikom *satyagraha* and for his editorship of Motilal Nehru's *The Independent* and Mahatma Gandhi's *Young India*.

On Joseph's return from London, he initially set up practice at Madras before shifting to Madurai. He hosted at his house in Madurai several leaders of the freedom struggle including Gandhi, C. Rajagopalachari, Srinivasa Iyengar and K. Kamaraj during their visits there. Subramania Bharati composed the '*Viduthalai*', a well-known patriotic song while staying at Joseph's residence.

In 1917, aged twenty-nine, Joseph was invited by Annie Besant to go to England along with her, Syed Hussain and B.V. Narasimhan to talk about home rule there. The British however foiled this bid, arresting them when the ship Besant had chartered reached Gibraltar; subsequently, deporting them back to India. When P. Varadarajulu Naidu was arrested for making a speech at the Victoria Edward Hall, George Joseph assisted C. Rajagopalachari, who appeared for Naidu in the case. Joseph was the leader of the Rowlatt *sstyagraha* in Madurai, organising meetings, fasts and hartals during the *satyagraha* and during the non-co-operation movement he relinquished his lucrative legal practice and joined the movement.

Joseph played an important role in setting up the trade union movement in Madurai to organise the textile mill workers there. The union's initial struggles resulted in higher wages and reduced work hours for the mill workers but soon the mill owners and the government came together to bring about a collapse of the union. Joseph edited the Nehru's Allahabad-based newspaper, *The Independent* during 1920-21 until his arrest on charges of sedition and the subsequent closure of the paper. He also succeeded Rajagopalachari to the editorship of Gandhi's *Young India* in 1923.

In 1929, Joseph contested the municipal elections in Madurai on a Congress ticket but lost. In July 1937, he was elected to the Central Legislative Assembly from Madurai-cum-Ramnad-Tirunelveli constituency.

Joseph died at the American Mission Hospital in Madurai on 5 March, 1938. He was fifty years old then. He is buried at the East Gate Cemetery in Madurai.

□

32

Gulab Kaur

(1890 – 1941)

Gulab Kaur was an Indian freedom fighter. In Manila, she joined the Ghadar Party, an organisation founded by Indian immigrants with the aim to liberate the Indian subcontinent from British rule.

Gulab Kaur kept vigil in disguise on the party's printing press. Posing as a journalist with a press pass in hand, she distributed arms to the Ghadar Party members. She also encouraged others to join the Ghadar Party by distributing Independence literature and delivering inspiring speeches to Indian passengers of ships.

Gulab Kaur, with about 50 other freedom Ghadrites of the Philippines, joined the '*S.S. Korea*' batch and sailed for India, changing at Singapore from '*S.S. Korea*' to '*Tosha Maru*'. After reaching India, she, with some other revolutionaries, was active in the villages of Kapurthala, Hoshiarpur and Jalandhar to mobilise the masses for armed revolution for the cause of the Independence of the country.

She was sentenced to two years in prison at Lahore, then in British-India and now in Pakistan, for seditious acts. There is a book available about Gulab Kaur, titled *Gadar di Dhee Gulaab Kaur* in Punjabi, written by S. Kesar Singh and published in 2014.

□

33

Harlal Singh Dhular

(3 February, 1901 – 21 March, 1982)

Harlal Singh was a freedom fighter and social worker who played a leading role in Shekhawati farmers' movement for abolition of *jagirdari* system. He was born on 3 February, 1901 at village Hanumanpura, near Mandawa in Jhunjhunu district of Rajasthan. He was of Dular *gotra*. His entire family was committed to the freedom movement. Pratibha Dular, present MLA from Nawalgarh constituency, is the grand daughter of Sardar Harlal Singh Dular.

Sardar Harlal Singh was evicted from his agricultural land and residence by the *jagirdars* for his acts of taking part in the *jagirdari* abolition movement. The *jagirdars* lodged a number of false charges against him, but he always succeeded in getting rid of them. The Mandawa Thakur attacked him in 1946, in a planned conspiracy. In this, a person was murdered and Harlal's brother received serious injuries on his head. All attempts by the *jagirdars* could not refrain him from participating in the freedom movement and he continued to lead the farmers and served the farmers through the Kisan Sabha and Praja Mandal.

'Pushkaradhiveshan' 1925, organised by the All India Jat Mahasabha was presided over by Maharaja Kishan Singh of Bharatpur. Sir Chhotu Ram, Madan Mohan Malviya, Chhajju Ram, etc. and farmers' leaders also attended. This function was organised at the initiative of Master Bhajan Lal Bijarnia of Ajmer-Merwara. The farmers from all parts of Shekhawati had come and they included Chaudhary Govind Ram, Kunwar Panne Singh Deorod, Ram Singh Bakhtawarpura, Chetram Bhadarwasi, Bhuda Ram Sangasi and Moti Ram Kotri. As a twenty-four year old boy, Harlal Singh also attended it. The Shekhawati farmers took two oaths at Pushkar, namely, they would work for the development of the society through elimination of social evils and by spreading education and subscribe to 'do or die' in matters of exploitation of farmers by the *jagirdars*.

There was a grand gathering of farmers under the banner of Jat Mahasabha in Jhunjhunu on 11-13 February, 1932. As many as 60,000 Jat farmers attended it. Thakur Deshraj camped at Jhunjhunu for fifteen days to make it a success. Farmers from all parts of India attended it. It was presided over by Rao Sahib Chaudhary Rishal Singh Rayees, who was escorted from tfhe station to the place of meeting on an elephant accompanied by a caravan of camels. This programme was of Jats but all the communities co-operated and participated. Kunwar Panne Singh Deorod welcomed this rally, whereas Vidyadhar Singh Sangasi welcomed the 'Jaipur Prantiya Jat Kshatriya Sabha' rallies. Though the *jagirdars* made all attempts to make the event a failure, but it proved a success. On the appeal of fund collection, the participant farmers donated their gold ornaments, which they were wearing. This was the first occasion of awakening among the Shekhawati farmers and proved a grand success. Sardar Harlal Singh and Chaudhary Ghasi Ram had travelled all over to work for its publicity and to spread its message. Some of the competent people were awarded Kshatriya titles; for example, Chaudhary Harlal Singh was awarded the title of 'Sardar', Ratan Singh of Bharatpur was given 'Kunwar' and Chaudhary Ram Singh was called 'Thakur'. Thus the Rajput monopoly over these titles vanished.

□

34

Kamaladevi Chattopadhya

(3 April, 1903 – 29 October, 1988)

Kamaladevi Chattopadhyay was an Indian social reformer and freedom activist. She is most remembered for her contribution to the Indian Independence movement, for being the driving force behind the renaissance of Indian handicrafts, handlooms, and theatre in Independent India and for upliftment of the socio-economic standard of Indian women by pioneering co-operation.

Several cultural institutions in India today exist because of her vision, including the National School of Drama, Sangeet Natak Akademi, Central Cottage Industries Emporium, and the Crafts Council of India. She emphasised the significant role which handicrafts and co-operative grassroot movements play in social and economic upliftment of the Indian people. To this end she withstood great opposition, both before and after Independence, from the power centres.

In 1974, she was awarded the Sangeet Natak

Akademi Fellowship, the highest honour conferred by the Sangeet Natak Akademi, India's national academy of music, dance & drama. She was conferred with Padma Bhushan and Padma Vibhushan by the Government of India in 1955 and 1987 respectively. Shortly after her marriage with Harin Chattopadhyay, Harin left for London, on his first trip abroad, and a few months later Kamaladevi joined him, where she joined Bedford College, University of London, and later received a diploma in Sociology.

She became the founding-member of the All-India Women's Conference (AIWC) and was its first organising secretary. At the same time, AIWC grew up to become a national organisation of repute, with branches and voluntary programmes run throughout the nation, and worked steadfastly for legislative reforms. During her tenure, she travelled extensively to many European nations and was inspired to initiate several social reforms and community welfare programmes, and set up educational institutions run for women and by women. Another shining example in this series was the founding of Lady Irwin College for Home Sciences – one of its kind college for women in its time, at New Delhi. Later, she was a part of the seven-member lead team, announced by Mahatma Gandhi, in the famous Salt Satyagraha (1930), to prepare salt at the Bombay beach-front. The only other woman volunteer of the team was Avantikabai Gokhale. Later, in a startling move, Kamaladevi went up to a nearby High Court and asked a magistrate present there whether he would be interested in buying the 'freedom salt' she had just prepared. On 26 January, 1930, she caught widespread media attention when in a scuffle, she clung to the Indian tricolor, to protect it.

Post-Independence Work

Independence of India brought Partition in its wake and Kamaladevi plunged into rehabilitation of refugees from Pakistan. Her first task was to set up the Indian Co-operative Union to help with rehabilitation and through the Union, she made plans for a township on co-operative basis. At length, Jawaharlal Nehru reluctantly gave her permission on the condition that she would not ask for State assistance, and so after much struggle, the township of Faridabad was set up, on the outskirts of Delhi to rehabilitate over 50,000 refugees from the North-West Frontier Province. She worked tirelessly in helping the refugees to establish new homes and find new professions – for this they were trained in new skills. She also helped set up health facilities in the new town.

The Government of India conferred on her the Padma Bhushan in 1955 and the Padma Vibhushan in 1987, which are among the most revered civilian awards of the Republic of India. She was awarded the Ramon Magsaysay Award in 1966 for 'community leadership'. In 1974, she was awarded the Sangeet Natak Akademi Fellowship, *Ratna Sadasya*, in recognition of her lifetime's work. The fellowship is the highest award of Sangeet Natak Akademi, India's national academy of music, dance and drama.

UNESCO honoured her with an award in 1977, for her contribution towards the promotion of handicrafts. Shantiniketan honoured her with the Desikottama, its highest award.

□

35

Kanaiyalal Maneklal Munshi

(30 December, 1887 – 8 February, 1971)

Kanaiyalal Maneklal Munshi, popularly known by his pen name, Ghanshyam Vyas, was an Indian Independence movement activist, politician, writer and educationist from Gujarat state. A lawyer by profession, he later became an author and politician. He is a well-known name in Gujarati literature. He founded the Bharatiya Vidya Bhavan, an educational trust, in 1938.

Due to the influence of Aurobindo, Munshi leaned towards the revolutionary group and got himself involved in the process of bomb-making. But after settling down in Bombay (now Mumbai), he joined the Indian Hhome Rrule movement and became secretary in 1915. In 1917, he became secretary of Bombay Presidency Association. In 1920, he attended the annual Congress session at Ahmedabad and was influenced by its president Surendranath Banerjee.

In 1927, he was elected to the Bombay Legislative Assembly but after the Bardoli *satyagraha*, he resigned, under the influence of Mahatma Gandhi. He participated in the Civil Disobedience movement in 1930 and was arrested for six months initially. After taking part in the second part of the same movement, he was arrested again and spent two years in the jail, in 1932. In 1934, he became secretary of Congress Parliamentary Board.

Munshi was elected again in the 1937 Bombay Presidency election and became Home Minister of Bombay Presidency. During his tenure as Home Minister, he suppressed the communal riots in Bombay. Munshi was again arrested, after he took part in an individual *satyagraha* in 1940. As the demand for Pakistan gathered momentum, he gave up non-violence and supported the idea of a civil war to compel the Muslims to give up their demand. He believed that the future of Hindus and Muslims lay in unity, in an *Akhand Hindustan*. He left Congress in 1941 due to dissent with Congress, but was invited back in 1946 by Mahatma Gandhi.

At the time of Post-Independent India, he was a part of several committees, including the Drafting Committee, Advisory Committee, Sub-committee on Fundamental Rights. Munshi presented his draft on Fundamental Rights to the Drafting Committee and sought for progressive rights to be made a part of Fundamental Rights. After India's Independence, Munshi, Sardar Patel and N.V. Gadgil visited Junagadh to stabilise the state with help of the Indian Army. In Junagadh, Patel declared the reconstruction of the historically important Somnath temple. Patel died before the reconstruction could be completed. Munshi became the main driving force behind the renovation of Somnath temple, even after Jawaharlal Nehru's opposition. Munshi was appointed diplomatic envoy and trade agent (Agent-General) to the princely state of Hyderabad, where he served until its accession to India in 1948. Munshi was on the ad hoc Flag Committee that selected the flag of India in August 1947, and on the committee which drafted the Constitution of India under the chairmanship of B.R. Ambedkar. Besides being a politician and educator, Munshi was also an environmentalist. He initiated the Van Mahotsav in 1950, when he was the Union Minister of Food and Agriculture, to increase the area under forest cover. Since then Van Mahotsav, a week-long festival of tree plantation, is organised every year in the month of July, all across the country and lakhs of trees are planted. Munshi served as the Governor of Uttar Pradesh from 1952 to 1957.

In 1959, Munshi separated from the Nehru-dominated (socialist) Congress Party and started the *Akhand Hindustan* movement. He believed in a strong Opposition, so along with Chakravarti Rajagopalachari, he founded the Swatantra Party, which was right-wing in its politics, pro-business, pro-free market economy and private property rights. The party enjoyed considerable success but eventually died out.

In August 1964, he chaired the meeting for the founding of the Hindu nationalist organisation Vishwa Hindu Parishad at Sandipini Ashram.

□

36

Kanaklata Barua

(22 December, 1924 – 20 September, 1942)

Kanaklata was also called Birbala and Shaheed (martyr) and was an activist in the Indian freedom struggle and an AISF leader who was shot dead by the British police while leading a procession bearing the national flag during the Quit India movement of 1942.

Barua was born in the Borangabari village of the undivided Darrang district of Assam as the daughter of Krishna Kanta and Karneshwari Barua. Her grandfather Ghana Kanta Barua was a famous hunter in Darrang. Her ancestors previously were Dolakasharia Barua, but later relinquished the Dolakakharia title and retained the Barua title. Her mother died when she was only five and her father, who remarried, died when she reached the age of thirteen. She went to school till Class III but then dropped out to take care of her younger siblings.

During the Quit India movement, Barua joined the Mrityu Bahini, a death squad comprising groups of youth from the Gohpur sub-division of Assam. On 20 September, 1942, the Bahini decided to hoist the national flag at the local police station. A procession of unarmed villagers led by Barua was ordained to do so. The police under Rebati Mahan Som, the officer in-charge of the police station, warned the procession of dire consequences if they proceeded with their plan. Undeterred by the police, the procession continued marching ahead when the police fired upon them. Barua was shot and the flag she was carrying with her was taken up by Mukunda Kakoti, who too was shot at. Both Barua and Kakoti were killed in the police action. Barua was only seventeen years of age at the time of her martyrdom.

The fast patrol vessel '*ICGS Kanaklata Barua* of the Indian Coast Guard, commissioned in 1997, was named after Barua. A life size statue of hers was unveiled at Gauripur in 2011. Her impassioned speech before her death remains a source of inspiration for many. She laid down her life for the freedom of the country at the age of seventeen years.

☐

37

Kaneganti Hanumanthu

(1870 – 22 February 1920)

Kaneganti Hanumanthu was a freedom fighter who rebelled against British rule and spearheaded the Palnadu rebellion against tax. He was executed by the British General Rutherford. He was born at Kolagutla in the Durgi Mandal, which is in Palnadu of Guntur district.

A local peasant leader, he refused to pay British taxes and participated in a revolt over the issue. He was killed while resisting the British police forces at the age of 30.

The Palnadu rebellion is attributed to Hanumanthu.

□

38

Kazinazrul Islam

(24 May, 1899 – 29 August, 1976)

Kazinazrul Islam was a Bengali poet, writer, musician, film actor and the national poet of Bangladesh. Popularly known as Nazrul, he produced a large body of poetry and music with themes that included religious devotion and rebellion against oppression. Nazrul's activism for political and social justice earned him the title of 'Bidrohi Kobi' (Rebel Poet). His compositions form the avant-garde music genre of Nazrul *geeti* (Music of Nazrul)

Born into a Bengali-Muslim Kazi family hailing from Burdwan district of Bengal Presidency (now in West Bengal), Nazrul Islam received religious education and as a young man worked as a muezzin at a local mosque. He learned about poetry, drama and literature while working with the rural theatrical group Letor Dal, Leto being a folk-song genre of West Bengal, usually performed by the people from Muslim community of the region.

His nationalist activism in India's Independence movement led to his frequent imprisonment by the colonial British authorities. While in prison, Nazrul wrote the *Rajbandir Jabanbandi* (Deposition of a Political Prisoner). His writings greatly inspired Bengalis of East Pakistan during the Bangladesh Liberation War.

Nazrul's writings explored themes, such as freedom, humanity, love and revolution. He opposed all forms of bigotry and fundamentalism, including religious, caste-based and gender-based. Nazrul returned to Calcutta on 15 December, 1953. On 30 June, 1962 Pramila died and Nazrul remained in intensive medical care. He stopped working due to his deteriorating health. On 24 May, 1972, the newly independent nation of Bangladesh brought Nazrul to live in Dacca with the consent of the Government of India. In January 1976, he was accorded the citizenship of Bangladesh.

□

39

K.E. Mammem

(31 July, 1921 – 26 July, 2017)

K.E. Mammem was an Indian freedom fighter. He was a follower of Mahatma Gandhi and K. Kelappan is often referred to as the Kerala Gandhi. Mammen was born into the Kandathil family on 31 July, 1921 as the sixth child of K.C. Eapen and Kunjandamma, at Trivandrum. His father was a manager at the National Quilon Bank and they lived opposite the Kerala Government Secretariat where freedom fighters used to converge to make speeches. Mammen was a staunch follower of Gandhian ideals and led an austere life. He remained unmarried.

He became president of the Travancore Students Federation while he was an intermediate student at College of Fine Arts, Trivandrum. During this period, he was jailed for urging students to join the freedom struggle, during a public meeting held at Thirunakkara. The famous 'Kozhencherry speech' by C. Kesavan inspired Mammen to dedicate himself to social causes.

The National Quilon Bank was closed by C.P. Ramaswami Iyer, who was the then Diwan of Travancore. Mammen's father, the brother of K.C Mammen Mappillai, was among the officials arrested and ended up dying in jail. He was expelled from the college for criticising the Diwan in a meeting and was refused admission to Maharaja's College, Ernakulam when he tried to continue his education there. He subsequently completed his intermediate course at St. Thomas College, Thrissur. He went to Madras Christian College for his bachelor's degree in 1940, but was soon expelled for participating in the Quit India movement.

During the period, Mahatma Gandhi invoked the youth to join the freedom struggle. Mammen was inspired by this and began working among the people of Thiruvalla and Kottayam. He was the candidate for the newly-formed Praja Socialist Party in the 1952 Travancore-Cochin Legislative Assembly election and ended up coming second by 500 votes. He received many accolades over his eventful life, including the Ramashramam Award, Lohi Vicharavedi Award and the TKV Foundation Award. Mammen was also actively involved in anti-liquor campaigns across the state of Kerala till his death.

He died on 26 July, 2017.

□

40

Khudiram Bose

(3 December, 1889 – 11 August, 1908)

Khudiram Bose was an Indian revolutionary from Bengal Presidency and he opposed British rule of India. For his role in the Muzaffarpur Conspiracy Case, along with Prafulla Chaki, he was sentenced to death and subsequently executed, making him one of the youngest martyrs of the India's Independence movement.

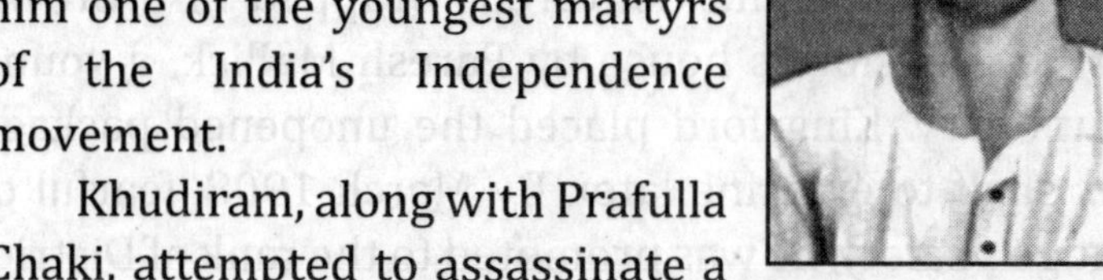

Khudiram, along with Prafulla Chaki, attempted to assassinate a British judge, Magistrate Douglas Kingsford, by throwing bombs on the carriage they suspected carried Magistrate Kingsford. However, he was seated in a different carriage and the throwing of bombs resulted in the deaths of two British women. Prafulla fatally shot himself before his arrest. Khudiram was arrested and underwent the trial for murder of the two women, ultimately being sentenced to death. He was one of the first freedom fighters in Bengal to be executed by the British.

At the time of his hanging, Khudiram was 18 years,

8 months, and 11 days, 10 hours old, making him one of the second youngest revolutionaries in India.

Mahatma Gandhi, however, denounced the violence, lamenting the deaths of the two innocent women. He stated that "the Indian people will not win their freedom through these methods. Bal Gangadhar Tilak, in his newspaper *Kesari*, defended the two young men and called for immediate *swaraj*. This was followed with the immediate arrest of Tilak by the British colonial government on charges of sedition.

First Attempt

The first attempt to kill Kingsford was in the form of a book bomb constructed by Hemchandra. An empty tin of Cadbury cocoa was packed with a pound of picric acid and three detonators. This was packed into a hollowed section of Herbert Broom's Commentaries on the Common Law and delivered, wrapped in a brown paper, to Kingsford's house by Paresh Mallick, a young revolutionary. Kingsford placed the unopened package on his shelf to examine later. By March 1908, fearful of the judge's safety, he was promoted to the rank of District Judge and transferred by the government to Muzaffarpur, Bihar. With him went his furniture, library and the book bomb.

Reconnaissance at Muzaffarpur

The Anushilan Samiti persisted in its attempt to kill Kingsford. In April, a two-man reconnaissance team visited Muzaffarpur, which included Prafulla Chaki. On their return, Hemchandra provided the bomb, which was composed of 6 ounces of dynamite, a detonator and a black powder fuse. Prafulla Chaki returned to Muzaffarpur with a new boy, Khudiram Bose.

Police Suspicion

The activities of Aurobindo Ghosh, Barindra Ghosh and their associates roused suspicion. The Calcutta police became aware of the plans to kill Kingsford. Commissioner F.L. Halliday's alerts to the Superintendent of Police in Muzaffarpur were ignored. However, four men were assigned to guard the magistrate's house. In the meantime, Khudiram Bose and Prafulla Chaki adopted the name of Haren Sarkar and Dinesh Chandra Roy respectively and took up residence in a charitable inn (*dharamshala*) run by Kishorimohan Bandyopadhyay. In the ensuing days, the duo monitored the activities and daily routine of their target. The two revolutionaries successfully hid their identities for over three weeks. The CID officer from Calcutta returned with a letter from the Superintendent of Muzaffarpur, a Mr Armstrong that the duo had not arrived.

On the evening of April 29, Khudiram and Prafulla reached their positions to execute their plan. Pretending to be schoolboys, they surveyed the Muzaffarpur Park situated opposite the British Club, frequented by Kingsford. However they were noticed by a constable.

Judgement

Khudiram was the only one to be alive among the two; his lone statement of a two-man team was the foundation for the entire case. Since all the legal arguments put forth by Narendra Kumar Basu were believed to be technically correct, it was hoped that for the sake of the law – about which the British prided themselves ad infinitum – Khudiram's life would, at least, be spared. But, on a historical day, the British judges confirmed the conviction and sentence and dismissed the appeal.

□

41

Koma Ram Bheem

(1900–1940)

Koma Ram was a revolutionary leader in British India and belonged to the Gond tribe. He, in association with other Gond leaders and communist revolutionaries, led a protracted low-intensity rebellion against the feudal Nizams of Hyderabad and the British Raj in the eastern part of the princely state, during the 1930s, contributing to the culmination of the Telangana rebellion of 1946.

He was killed by armed policemen in 1940, subsequently lionised as a symbol of rebellion and eulogised in Adivasi and Telugu folklore. Bheem is deified as a pen in Gond culture and is credited for coining the slogan, *'Jal, Jangal, Zameen'* (Water, Forest, Land) which symbolised a sentiment against encroachment and exploitation. It has been adopted by Adivasi movements as 'a call to action'. He is also closely associated with the movement for Telangana statehood.

Komaram Bheem was one a leader of the Gond

rebellion but was lionised as its symbol following his death and over the years, eulogised in Adivasi and Telugu folk-songs. Bheem has been deified among the animistic Gond Adivasi community through the worship of Bheemal Pen. His death anniversary is commemorated by the Gonds every year on *Aswayuja Powrnami*, where an event is organised at Jodeghat, the place of his death and his centre of operations during the rebellion. His aides, Bhadu master and Maru master, are considered to have been instrumental in lionising him following his death, in order to motivate the demoralised combatants.

Following the death of Bheem, the Hyderabad state employed the Austrian ethnologist Christoph von Fürer-Haimendorf to study the causes of the rebellion. Haimendorf's work enabled the enactment of the Hyderabad Tribal Areas Regulation 1356 *Fasli* in 1946. Haimendorf had remarked at the time that "rebellions of aboriginal tribesmen against the authority of the government are among the most tragic conflicts between ruler and ruled" and that "it is always a hopeless struggle of the weak against the strong, the illiterate and uninformed against the organised power of a sophisticated system. The rebellion itself persisted for years after his death till it merged with the Telangana rebellion – a peasants' uprising led by the communists against the Nizam.

Bheem's legacy was largely ignored in the mainstream beyond the folk-culture of the impoverished Adivasis of central-east India and the Telangana movement in Andhra Pradesh. His marginalised status in Indian mainstream history contrasted with his idolisation as a revolutionary figure among the Adivasis, for whom he became an exemplification of their own marginalised and exploited status in India even after Independence. The slogan of *Jal, Jangal, Zameen*, symbolising a sentiment against encroachment and exploitation, has been adopted by Adivasi communities, particularly the Gonds for their social and political struggles, including as a war cry in the Naxalite-Maoist insurgency. In popular culture, the film 'Komaram Bheem' (1990) directed by Allani Sridhar, was created, based on his life and won two Nandi Awards.

In the 21st century, with growing support and prominence of the demand for the new state of Telangana – the legacy of Bheem – was brought back into the spotlight and began featuring in the mainstream political discourse and rhetoric. In 2011, the Andhra Pradesh government announced the construction of a dam and reservoir named Sri Komaram Bheem Project and the installation of his statue at Tank Bund Road in the city of Hyderabad. Following the establishment of the Telangana state in 2014, the state government allocated Rs. 25 crore (equivalent to Rs. 34 crore or US$4.5 million in 2020) for the construction of a Komaram Bheem museum on tribal history at Jodeghat and a memorial at Jodeghat hill-rock. The museum and memorial were inaugurated in 2016, and in the same year, the Adilabad district was reorganised with part of it carved out as Komaram Bheem district. The location near Jodeghat has become a major tourism destination in Telangana.

In 2018, S.S. Rajamouli, the director of Bahubali series of films, announced the film RRR which would incorporate Komaram Bheem and his contemporary

Alluri Sitarama Raju as characters. The plot, being a work of fiction, depicts a friendship between them and takes place in the less documented part of their lives, in the 1920s.

□

42

Kushal Konwar

(21 March, 1905 – 15 June, 1943)

Kushal Konwar was a freedom fighter from Assam and he happened to be the only martyr in India to be hanged during last phase of the Quit India movement of 1942-43.

Kushal Konwar was born in 21 March, 1905 at Balijan near Sarupathar in the modern district of Golaghat in Assam. His family descended from the royal family of Ahom kingdom and used the surname 'Konwar', which was later abandoned. Kushal attended the Bezbaruah School. In 1921, while still at school, he was inspired by Gandhi's call for non-co-operation movement and took an active part in it. Inspired by Gandhi's ideals of *swaraj*, truth and *ahimsa*, Konwar set up a primary school at Bengmai and served as its honorary teacher. Later, he joined the Balijan Tea Estate as a clerk and worked there for a while. However, the spirit of Independence and call of Mahatma Gandhi inspired him to dedicate himself wholeheartedly in the Independence movement. He organised the Congress Party and led the people of Sarupathar area in a *satyagraha* and non-co-operation movement against the British. He was elected the president of the Sarupathar Congress Committee.

On 8 August, 1942, the Congress Working Committee, in its meeting in Bombay, passed the 'Quit India' resolution. This resolution demanded complete withdrawal of the British from the Indian soil. Mahatma Gandhi gave the call of 'do or die' to the people of India. The British reacted by arresting Mahatma and all the Congress leaders were put in jails. Across India, this sparked a widespread mass movement against the British. Cutting across caste, creed and religion, people came out to the streets, shouting the slogan of '*Vande Mataram*'. In spite of Gandhi's appeal for peaceful non-co-operation and *dharna*, in many regions the movement erupted in violence with people burning offices and damaging government properties, disrupting road, rail and telecommunication networks.

Some people of Assam also spontaneously joined this historic movement of 1942. Two of the leaders of the Assam Pradesh Congress, Gopinath Bordoloi and Siddhinath Sarma, were arrested by the British in Dhubri while returning from Bombay after attending the Congress Working Committee meeting. Other Congress leaders, such as Bishnuram Medhi, Bimala Prasad Chaliha, Md. Tayebulla, Omeo Kumar Das, Debeswar Sarma, etc., were arrested from different parts of Assam and thrown into jails. Assam too burned like the rest of India and many people who had left the path of non-violence engaged in violence.

On 10 October, 1942, hidden in the thick fog of early morning, some people removed a few sleepers from the railway track near Sarupathar in Golaghat district. A military train passing by derailed and many British and American soldiers lost their lives.The British Army immediately cordoned the area and started an operation to catch the culprits. Innocent people of the area were rounded up, beaten and harassed. The British police participated in this reign of terror in which people were beaten up and arrested.

Accusing Kushal Konwar as the chief conspirator of the train sabotage, the British police arrested him. An ardent follower of Gandhiji and his principle of non-violence, Kushal was ignorant about the sabotage plan and action. He was innocent but the police charged him as the mastermind of the train sabotage. He was brought from Golaghat and lodged in the Jorhat Jail on 5 November, 1942.

In the court of C.M. Humphrey, Kushal Konwar was declared guilty, though there was not a single proof against him. Kushal was sentenced to death by hanging. He accepted the verdict with dignity. When his wife, Prabhavati visited him in the Jorhat Jail, he told her that he was proud that God has selected him to be the only one among the thousands of prisoners to give the supreme sacrifice for the country. Kushal spent his remaining days in the death row cell of Jorhat Jail in prayers and reading the *Gita*.

At dawn on 15 June, 1943 at 4:30 a.m., Kushal Konwar was hanged in Jorhat Jail. He sacrificed his life, knowing, as Mahatma said: "He alone can be a true *satyagrahi* who knows the art of living and dying."

☐

43

Lakshmi Sehgal

(24 October, 1914 – 23 July, 2012)

Lakshmi Sehgal was a revolutionary of the Indian Independence movement, an officer of the Indian National Army and the Minister of Women's Affairs in the Azad Hind government. Sehgal is commonly referred to in India as Captain Lakshmi in reference to her rank when taken prisoner in Burma during the Second World War.

Sehgal was born as Lakshmi Swaminathan in Malabar, Kerala on 24 October, 1914 to S. Swaminathan, a lawyer who practised criminal law at Madras High Court, and A.V. Ammukutty, better known as Ammu Swaminathan, a social worker and Independence activist from an aristocratic Nair family, known as 'Vadakkath' family of Anakkara in Palghat, Kerala. She is the elder sister of Mrinalini Sarabhai.

Sahgal studied in Queen Mary's College and later chose to study medicine and received an MBBS degree from Madras Medical College, in 1938. A year later, she received her diploma in gynaecology and obstetrics. She worked as a doctor in the Government Kasturba Gandhi Hospital located at Triplicane, Chennai.

In 1940, she left for Singapore after the failure of her marriage to pilot P.K.N. Rao. During her stay at Singapore, she met some members of Subhas Chandra Bose's Indian National Army.

In 1942, during the surrender of Singapore by the British to the Japanese, Sehgal aided wounded prisoners of war, many of whom were interested in forming an Indian Independence Army. Singapore at that time had several nationalist Indians working there, including K.P. Kesava Menon, S.C. Guha and N. Raghavan, who formed a Council of Action. Their Indian National Army, or Azad Hind Fauj, however, received no firm commitments or approval from the occupying Japanese forces regarding their participation in the war.

It was against this backdrop that Subhas Chandra Bose arrived in Singapore on 2 July, 1943. Lakshmi had heard that Bose was keen to draft women into the organisation and requested a meeting with him from which she emerged with a mandate to set up a women's regiment, to be called the Rani of Jhansi regiment. Women responded enthusiastically to join the all-women brigade and Dr. Lakshmi Swaminathan became Captain Lakshmi, a name and identity that would stay with her for life.

The INA marched into Burma with the Japanese Army in December 1944, but by March 1945, with the tide of war turning against them, the INA leadership decided to beat a retreat before they could enter Imphal. Captain Lakshmi was arrested by the British Army in

May 1945; she remained in Burma until March 1946, when she was sent to India – at a time when the INA trials in Delhi heightened popular discontent with and hastened the end of colonial rule.

In 1971, Sehgal joined the Communist Party of India (Marxist) and represented the party in the Rajya Sabha. During the Bangladesh crisis, she organised relief camps and medical aid in Calcutta for refugees, who streamed into India from Bangladesh. She was one of the founding members of All India Democratic Women's Association in 1981 and led many of its activities and campaigns. She led a medical team to Bhopal after the gas tragedy in December 1984, worked towards restoring peace in Kanpur following the anti-Sikh riots of 1984 and was arrested for her participation in a campaign against the Miss World competition at Bangalore in 1996. She was still seeing patients regularly at her clinic in Kanpur, in 2006, at the age of 92.

In 2002, four Leftist parties – the Communist Party of India, the Communist Party of India (Marxist), the Revolutionary Socialist Party and the All India Forward Bloc – nominated Sehgal as a candidate in the presidential elections. She was the sole opponent of A.P.J. Abdul Kalam, who emerged victorious.

On 19 July, 2012, Sahgal suffered a cardiac arrest and died on 23 July, 2012 at 11:20 a.m. at the age of 97, in Kanpur. Her body was donated to Ganesh Shankar Vidyarthi Memorial Medical College for medical research. □

44

Lokenath Bal

(8 March, 1908 – 4 September, 1964)

Lokenath Bal was an Indian Independence activist and a member of the armed resistance movement led by Surya Sen. He carried out the Chittagong armoury raid in 1930.

Later, he joined the Indian National Congress. After the Indian Independence, he worked as an administrative officer in the Calcutta Corporation till his death. Lokenath Bal was born in Dhorla village of Chittagong district in Bengal province of British India. His father's name was Prankrishna Bal. On 18 April, 1930, a group of revolutionaries led by him took over the AFI armoury. Later, on 22 April, 1930, he led another gunfight with a combined force comprising the British army and the British police. His younger brother Harigopal Bal (Tegra) and another 11 revolutionaries died in this gunfight. He was able to escape and reach Chandernagore, a French territory. He and Ganesh Ghosh were arrested on 1 September, 1930 after a gunfight with the British police. Jiban Ghoshal alias Makhan, his young associate, died in this gunfight. He was sentenced to transportation for life on 1 March, 1932 and sent to the Cellular Jail in Port Blair. After his release in 1946, he joined the Radical Democratic Party founded by Manabendra Nath Roy. Later, he joined the Indian National Congress.

Bal was the second Deputy Commissioner of the Calcutta Corporation from 1 May, 1952 to 19 July, 1962. He was promoted as its first Deputy Commissioner on 20 July, 1962 and remained in office till his death in Calcutta on 4 September, 1964.

□

45

Lothoo Nitharwal

(1804-1855)

Lothoo Nitharwal was a revolutionary freedom fighter of Rajasthan. He struggled all his life to end British rule in India and to get the people freedom from exploitation by *samants* and then to establish democracy. He was a socialistic radical thinker and pioneer of social reforms at a time when one could not even think of freedom. He was born in 1804 to a Hindu Jat family of Nitharwalgotra in the town Ringas of Shekhawati region in Rajasthan.

Lothoo did not get formal school education as *jagirdars* prohibited the sons of farmers from studying during British Raj. There was a severe penalty for such action. Even the touching of *Vedas* and *Puranas* by farming communities was treated as an offence. The farmers were badly oppressed and exploited by *jagirdars*. Lathoo could get some knowledge of Hindi without being noticed by the *jagirdars*. He also managed to get a little knowledge of English too.

The family of Lathoo was simple, self-respecting and fearless. Lathoo did not like the slavery practiced by *jagirdars*. One day a son of Thakur of Ringas, popularly called Kunwar, was going on a horse. He saw Lothoo passing by his horse but not saluting the Kunwar. This irked the Kunwar who climbed down the horse and started abusing Lothoo and even slapped Lothoo. Lothoo, in turn, without showing any anger, picked the Kunwar by hand, slapped him and threw him in air. The Kunwar died on the spot. Lothoo narrated this incident to his parents. The incident sent alarms amongst the *jagirdars*. The parents of Lothoo thought it better to move from Ringas to another place to avoid any confrontation. Lothoo's sister was married in a village called Bathot, in a Kalwaniya family. So Lothoo along with his parents migrated from Ringas to village Bathot and started living with their relatives. The Ringas Thakur did not dare to come to Bathot and penalise Lothoo.

Lothoo had a very strong, tall and sturdy personality. He was of 6 feet and 11 inches in height and had 160 kg weight. His neck was one foot long. He was an excellent horse rider. He had a horse named Navlakha, which was his most beloved animal. He was an intelligent, tactful and a visionary person. He was a brave warrior, full of confidence. He was not afraid of *samants*, Rajas and British Raj. He could never be captured or arrested. He could play the role of various characters successfully and befool anybody. His judgement in various situations, keeping in view the local conditions, was so perfect that he could implement his plans in extremely dangerous situations. He never failed in his plans. He was against the oppression by *jagirdars* and a justice-loving person.

He used to settle local disputes so amicably that he was popularly known as Chief Justice in the villages around Sikar. He was a socialistic thinker and pioneer of social reforms.

Lothoo was very much impressed by bravery of Maharana Pratap. He had great respect for Veer Tejaji of Dhaulya Kshatriya *gotra*. Tejaji was a folk-deity of Rajasthan and farmers, while cultivating fields, sang his songs. Lothoo used to sing Tejaji's song with such force that it could be heard in a radius of 8 kms. He was also a follower of Chhatrapati Shivaji. Others who impressed him were Veer Gokula and Maharaja Suraj Mal of Bharatpur princely state.

Rao Raja Laxman Singh was the ruler of Sikar during those days. In order to avoid dispute within his queens, Patwi Rani and Veera Rani, he had constructed the fort of Laxmangarh in 1805, at the site of village Bedgaon. Laxmangarh had become a big centre of trade. The Bidawat Rajputs used to loot the traders. Due to terror of Lothoo, the traders at many times would send money to him for protection. Lothoo used to loot the towns of Bikaner, Nagaur and Jodhpur in Rajasthan. The booty was distributed amongst the poor people.

Rao Raja Laxman Singh of Sikar died in 1833. His son Pratap Singh became the successor of Sikar state. He was not mature enough. Pratap Singh had complained to British about the unrest in Shekhawati region. The British sent Col. Locket in 1831-32 to Sikar and give a report about unrest in Shekhawati areas. He went and later suggested that if proper steps were not initiated, the British rule in Shekhawati might be in trouble. So on his advice, the British Government formed an army named Shekhawati Brigade, in 1831-32. This army included British soldiers as well as Indian soldiers who were acquainted with the area. Indian soldiers were Rajputs who were loyal to British Raj. In 1836-37, the Shekhawati Brigade was transferred to Jaipur state and strengthened to curb the revolt in Shekhawati.

Dungar Singh was on the post of *risaldar* during Laxman Singh's regime and in the horse army of Shekhawati Brigade. He developed differences with British officers due to their behaviour with Indians and left the job. He came to Bathot and occupied the Bathot fort in 1834. Thakur Jawahar Singh was a cousin-brother of Thakur Dungar Singh and he became the successor of Thakur Vijay Singh of Patoda, as he had no son.

The exploitation by British Raj was increasing day by day. Bathot was also looted due to which the fire of revolt spread in this area. British Raj looked Dungar Singh and Jawahar Singh with suspicion. Both the Sardars were aware of the influence and power of Lothoo. So they invited Lothoo to the Bathot fort and asked for his co-operation in revolt against British Raj. Lothoo agreed upon the proposal and all decided to send the British out of India.

Paswania brothers were creating problems for Rao Pratap Singh. So he converted 50 villages of Singrawat *pargana* to Khalsa villages. The chieftain of this *pargana* was Mukund Singh. Mukund Singh complained about it to the British, but it was rejected. This made Mukund Singh a rebel. Bathot, Patoda and Garauda *samants* supported Mukund Singh. The British Army under the leadership of Major Ladlo entered Sikar and sent Lala Hardayal and Hanumant Singh with an army to occupy

Singrawat fort. The British Army attacked Singrawat fort and destroyed it. Mukund Singh, Lothoo, Jawahar Singh and Karana Meena escaped in the night and looted the fort of Sikar the very same day. Mukund Singh, Chiman Singh and Hukum Singh migrated to Marwar and Lothoo came to Bathot. Singrawat fort fell to Rao Pratap Singh.

After the fall of Singrawat fort to the British, their next targets were Bathot, Patoda, Sutot, Magloona and Gadauda. The British Army later attacked Sutot fort and occupied it without much resistance.

The biggest enemies of British Raj in Rajasthan were the *samants* of Bathot and Patauda. The occupation of Sutot fort by British sent waves of worry to the *samant* of Bathot. In a small fort of Bathot, Dungar Singh, Jawahar Singh, Lothoo and Karana Meena with other trusted Sardars gathered to plan the resistance of attack on Bathot. Lothoo suggested that looking at their meagre resources, they should loot horses and arms from the British Army. Dungar Singh and Lathoo attacked a British battalion thereafter. They captured arms and some good horses from the battalion and let other horses free. British officer, Major Forester was shocked to learn about this loot. He chased them but could not capture them.

Money was the biggest problem for the rebels to fight the British forces. The rebels used to keep their money deposited with Seth Ganediwala, who supported the rebellions.

They sent a message to the Seths of Ramgarh (Shekhawati) to provide financial support for the movement against British but they refused it on the pretext of famine in Rajasthan at that time. On receiving this reply from Ramgarh Seths, Lothoo and Dungar Singh decided to gather booty from the rich Seths. Lothoo and Karana Meen changed their appearance and entered Ramgarh as impersonators. They went to the *haveli* of a big Seth and gathered information about the caravan, which was supposed to carry huge wealth and stocks of grains for the British in Ajmer. They came back to Bathot. Lothoo and Dungar Singh attacked the caravan on a predestined place when the above caravan was camping at Andawali valley of Aravalli Hills. Lothoo and Dungar Singh attacked the caravan and looted it. The food-grain was distributed amongst the villagers. The British Government viewed this incidence seriously. Dungar Singh, Sanwata Meena and Lothoo were declared as dacoits and awards were declared on their arrest with an assurance of a job.

Lothoo had one brother, named Pema and one sister. Lothoo's sister was married in village Bathot in a Kalwania family. Lothoo's wife was a brave lady who gave birth to one son named Kushala Ram Nitharwal. It is said he was as brave as Lothoo.

□

46
Maruthu Pandiyar

Maruthu Pandiyar were diarchal kings of Sivagangai, Tamil Nadu towards the end of the 18th century. They were known for fighting against the East India Company and were finally executed by the Company after being captured. Periya and Chinna Marudhu, sons of Mookiah Palaniappan Servai, was natives of Mukkulam, near Narikudi, which was 18 miles away from Aruppukottai. Their mother Anandhayee alias Ponnathal was native of Pudhupatti, near Sivagangai. Both the brothers were born at Mukkulam in the year 1748 and 1753 respectively. The first son was named as Vellai Maruthu alias Periya Maruthu and the second son as Chinna Maruthu.

In 1772, Muhammad Ali Khan Wallajah, (the Nawab of Arcot) killed Muthuvaduganatha Thevar over his refusal to pay taxes. However, Marudhu Pandiyar and Queen Velunachiyar escaped and stayed with Gopala Nayak at Virupatchi for eight years. After this, an alliance of kingdoms led by the Pandiyar attacked Sivagangai and retook it in 1789. Both Maruthu Pandiyars were given high positions in the kingdom.

They were good at aerodynamics and craftsmanship and is said to have invented the *valari*, a variant of the boomerang.

The Maruthu Pandiyars planned to war against the East India Company. They gave the protection to Velunachiyar, who was temporarily seeking refuge from the chaos of war. They along with the war leader Sivagangai and many of their family members were captured at Cholapuram and were killed at Tiruppattur. They were hanged in the fort of Tirupputhur, which is now in Sivaganga district, Tamil Nadu, on 24 October, 1801. Maruthu Pandiyars is located at Sivagangai .

□

47
Matangini Hazra

(17 November, 1870 – 29 September, 1942)

Matangini was born in the small village of Hogla, near Tamluk, in 1869 and just because she was the daughter of a poor peasant, she did not receive formal education. She was married early and became widowed at the age of eighteen without bearing any offspring. In 1905, she became actively interested in the India's Independence movement as a Gandhian. A notable feature of the freedom struggle in Midnapore was the participation of women. In 1932, she took part in the Civil Disobedience movement and was arrested

for breaking the Salt Act. She was promptly released, but protested for the abolition of the tax. Arrested again, she was incarcerated for six months at Baharampur. After being released, she became an active member of the Indian National Congress and took to spinning her own *khadi* cloth. In 1933, she attended the sub-divisional Congress conference at Serampore and was injured in the ensuing baton charge by the police. As part of the Quit India movement, members of the Congress planned to take over the various police stations of Midnapore district and other government offices. This was to be a step in overthrowing the British government in the district and establishing an independent Indian state. Hazra, who was 72 years old at the time, led a procession of six thousand supporters, mostly women volunteers, with the purpose of taking over the Tamluk police station. When the procession reached the outskirts of the town, they were ordered to disband under Section 144 of the Indian Penal Code by the Crown police .As she stepped forward, Hazra was shot once. Apparently, she had stepped forward and appealed to the police not to open fire at the crowd.

□

48

N.G. Ranga

(7 November, 1900 – 9 June, 1995)

Gogineni Ranga Nayukulu, also known as N.G. Ranga, was an Indian freedom fighter, classical liberal, parliamentarian and farmer leader. He was the founding president of Swatantra Party. He was an exponent of the peasant's philosophy and considered the father of the Indian Peasant Movement. Ranga was born in Nidubrolu village of Guntur district of Andhra Pradesh. He went to school in his native village and graduated from the Andhra-Christian College, Guntur. He received a B.Litt. in Economics from the University of Oxford, in 19266. On his return to India, he took up teaching as Professor of Economics at Pachaiyappa's College, Madras (Chennai).

Ranga joined the freedom movement on getting inspired by Gandhi's clarion call in 1930. He led the Ryot agitation in 1933. He wrote a book, *Bapu Blesses*, regarding his discussions with Gandhi.

He wrote many other books, like *Credo of World*

Peasantry, Economic Organisation of Indian Villages and *Indian Adult Education Movement,* which are illustrative of a brilliant erudite ability and diverse interests.

Ranga served the Indian Parliament for six decades, from 1930 to 1991. He died on 9 June, 1995. Prime Minister P.V. Narasimha Rao condoled the death of Prof. Ranga. He said that in the passing away of Prof. Ranga, the country had lost an outstanding parliamentarian and a champion of public causes and of the rural peasantry. Prof. Ranga served as a Member of Parliament for a record number of 60 years and found a place in the *Guinness Book of World Records* .The Andhra Pradesh government declared a three-day state mourning.

□

49

Nihal Singh Takshak

(4 May, 1863 – 20 July, 1901)

Nihal Singh Takshak was a politician from the village of Bhagwi, Punjab (now in Haryana), India. In 1939, he founded the Jind State Praja Mandal political party. He was first MLA from Jind, following the election of 1937. [citation needed] He was also an Education Inspector with Birla Institute, Pilani. He started Basic Education School with help of Birla Trust in every village of Luharu-Jind state, now district Bhiwani.

Having served as a minister in the government of Jind, Takshak was involved in the wrangling that resulted from the formation in 1948 of the short-lived state known as the Patiala and East Punjab States Union (PEPSU). There were three organisations vying to hold the reins of power – Akali Dal, Lok Sewak Dal and the Praja Mandal. The latter suffered from internal rivalries and Takshak, along with Zail Singh, Seth Ram Nath and Harcharan Singh, were encouraged to split from it by forming the Pepsu Pradesh Congress Committee. They entered the government of Gian Singh Rarewala, which was sworn in on 13 January, 1949. He became Education and Finance Minister for the new state. Later, in 1953, he was among a group of MLAs who rebelled against the Indian National Congress government of Raghbir Singh, causing it to collapse and Rarewala once again to assume power. *The Hindu* has said that he was the first example of a politician changing allegiance in India. The action was later to stigmatise him. He founded Birhi Teacher Training School and Art Craft Teacher Training in Arya Hindi Mahavidyalaya, Charkhi Dadri. A statue in his honour was unveiled at Bhagwi, in 2007.

□

50

Pandurang Mahadev Bapat

(12 November, 1880 – 28 November, 1967)

Pandurang Mahadev Bapat, popularly known as Senapati Bapat, was a prominent figure in the Indian Independence movement. He acquired the title of Senapati, meaning 'commander', as a consequence of his leadership during the Mulshi *satyagraha*. In 1977, the Indian Government issued a postage stamp to commemorate him.

During his stay in Britain, he was associated with India House, where he spent considerable time learning bomb-making skills, instead of pursuing his official studies. He became associated at this time with the Savarkar brothers, Vinayak and Ganesh. Bapat, who had plans of blowing up the Houses of Parliament in London, took his skills back to India and passed them on to others.

While in hiding, after the Alipore bombing of 1908, Bapat travelled all over the country and discovered that the majority of Indian population did not realise that their country was under foreign rule. At this point, his focus shifted from overthrowing the British government to educating the population. In 1912, he was arrested in connection with the bombing and was sentenced to be imprisoned. He was freed by 1915 and was a 'seasoned revolutionary', according to Richard Cashman. He had joined the staff of *Mahratta* and was one of several influential figures from the Poona area to align with Bal Gangadhar Tilak's attempts to establish local organisations supporting the cause of Indian Independence.

He shifted to Gandhian philosophy and re-aligned himself with Gandhi's vision of *swaraj*. In late 1920, following the death of Tilak and despite having been a fervent supporter of Tilak's vision, he drifted apart. This was a considerable shift, given his firebrand nature and willingness to use violence. But, although he took the Gandhian oath of non-violence, he remained willing to use force when he thought it necessary. From 1921, Bapat led the three-year farmers' protest (*satyagraha*) against the construction of the Mulshi Dam by

the Tata Company. Ghanshyam Shah considers this to be "the first recorded organised struggle against [forced] displacement" caused by an irrigation project. The company had initially dug test trenches on land without obtaining permission and the farmers, who were mostly tenants, objected in fear of losing their lands. The dam was eventually constructed and thus the protest ultimately failed. Compensation for lands submersed by the dam's construction was eventually arranged but was given to the landlords, rather than to the tenants. Although *satyagrahas* are intended to be non-violent, Bapat was jailed for vandalism of the construction project: rather than be captured for this, he turned himself in. His third jail sentence was for speaking at a public gathering held by Subhas Chandra Bose.

Major public roads in Pune and Mumbai have been named in his honour and he featured in issue 303 of the *Amar Chitra Katha* comic book series in 1984. In 1977, the Government of India issued a postage stamp to commemorate him.

On 15 August, 1947, India's Independence Day, Bapat was given the honour of raising the Indian national flag over the city of Poona for the first time.

□

51

Parbati Giri

(19 January 1926 – 1995)

Parbati Giri was daughter of Dhananjay Giri. Nicknamed as 'Mother Teresa of Western Orissa', she was a prominent female freedom fighter from Orissa. The women freedom fighters of Orissa played a significant role in the Indian freedom struggle.

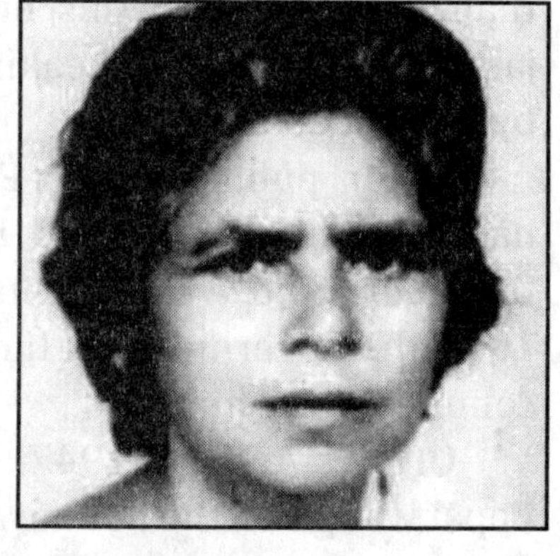

Due to her anti-British Government activities, she was imprisoned for two years. Parbati Giri was just sixteen years old when she was in the forefront of the agitation following Mahatma Gandhi's 'Quit India' call. She continued to serve the nation socially after Independence. She opened an orphanage at Paikmal village and devoted the rest of her life to the welfare of orphans. Her uncle Ramchandra Giri was a Congress leader and Samlaipadar village was an important place of gathering for the nationalists. She was influenced to work as a freedom fighter, since she would sit in and listen to the meetings held with her uncle. In 1940, Parbati began travelling for the Congress to Bargarh, Sambalpur, Padampur, Panimara, Ghens and other places. She trained villagers, teaching them how to spin and weave *khadi*. From 1942 she campaigned for the 'Quit India' movement and was arrested several times but since she was a minor, the police had to release her. She was finally arrested when she invaded the SDO's office at Bargar. She was sentenced to two years' rigorous imprisonment at Sambalpur Jail. At Bargarh Court she staged an agitation to persuade the lawyers to boycott the court in defiance of the British.

After Independence, she completed her schooling at the Prayag Mahila Vidyapith at Allababad in 1950. Four years later, she joined Rama Devi in her relief work. In 1955, she joined an American project to improve the health and hygiene of the people of Sambalpur district. She started an *ashram* for women and orphans and called it the Kasturba Gandhi Matruniketan at Nrusinghanath and another home for the destitute, called Dr. Santra Bal Niketan at Birasingh Gar under Jujomura block in Sambalpur district. She worked for jail improvement and leprosy eradication. The Department of Social Welfare of the Government of India awarded her a prize in 1984. □

52

Pazhassi Raja

(3 January, 1753 – 30 November, 1805)

Pazhassi Raja was known as Kerala Varma, as Cotiote Rajah and as Pychy Rajah. He was a warrior Hindu prince and de facto head of the kingdom of Kottayam, otherwise known as Cotiote, in Malabar between 1774 and 1805. His struggles with the British East India Company led to Cotiote war. He is popularly known as Kerala *simham* ('lion of Kerala') on account of his martial exploits.

Pazhassi Raja was a member of the western branch of the Kottayam royal clan. When Hyder Ali of the kingdom of Mysore occupied Malabar, in 1773, the Raja of Kottayam sought political asylum at Kallara near Vikom, in Kottayam district of Kerala. Pazhassi Raja, the fourth prince in line for succession to the throne, during this period, became one of the de facto heads of state, surpassing several older royal contenders. He fought a war of resistance against the Mysore Army, from 1774 to 1793. On account of his refusal to flee and due to his effective resistance to Mysoreans, he gained firm support from his subjects.

In 1792, after the third Anglo-Mysore war, the East India Company imposed control in Kottayam in violation of an earlier agreement of 1790 which had recognised its independence. Vira Varma, to whom Raja was a nephew, was appointed by the East India Company authorities as the Raja of Kottayam. To meet revenue targets fixed by Company authorities, Vira Varma ordered an exorbitant tax to be collected from the peasantry and this move was met, in 1793, by a mass resistance led by Pazhassi Raja, who had always been opposed to the Company's rule. In 1796, the Company made an attempt to arrest Pazhassi Raja, but he evaded capture and instead fought back, using guerilla warfare. After a string of serious setbacks, the Company sought peace in 1797. The conflict was renewed in 1800 over a dispute on Wayanad and after a five-year-long war of insurgency, Pazhassi Raja was killed on 30 November, 1805 in a gun-fight at Mavila Thodu (small body of water), on the present-day Kerala-Karnataka border.

Pazhassi Raja's warfare with Mysore troops can be divided into two phases, based on the rulers of the kingdom of Mysore. First phase lasted from 1773 to 1782 during which time, the Mysore ruler was Hyder Ali. The second phase extended from 1784 to 1793 and during this phase he fought the troops of Tipu Sultan, son and successor of Hyder Ali.

In 1773, Hyder Ali marched into Malabar for the second time, for non-payment of tributes from the Rajas (kings) of Malabar, as agreed after war in 1768. Most of the Rajas of Malabar, along with many Naduvazhis or vassals fled to seek political asylum in Travancore. Princes and younger noblemen, who refused to flee the invasion, organised resistance. The Malabari partisans made excellent use of the wooded hills that covered most of Malabar during this rebellion.

In 1774, at the age of 21, Pazhassi Raja took over the throne to replace his uncle, who had fled to Travancore. He vowed to resist Hyder Ali's troops and stayed in Kottayam, where he gathered a force and began guerrilla battles against the troops of Mysore as he had neither guns nor troops enough to face them in an open battle. He set up a large number of bases in the nearly impenetrable forested mountains of Puralimala and Wayanad and repeatedly inflicted severe minor losses on the Mysore Army in Kottayam as well as in Wayanad.

Once the true Raja of Kottayam had fled, three royals rose to power in Kottayam. The nephew of the escaped Raja, named Vira Varma and his nephews Ravi Varma and Pazhassi Raja, now took over the reins of government. Vira Varma was skilled in political intrigue and manipulation whereas Ravi Varma was too incompetent to play any serious political role and hence his role was nominal. Pazhassi Raja become the most powerful figure in Kottayam, much to the chagrin of his uncle Vira Varma. Hence Vira Varma played a series of power games, aiming to check the growing clout of his nephew. So the relationship between Vira Varma and Pazhassi Raja was one of enmity right from the onset.

The military situation was grim for Pazhassi Raja and his troops, in 1774, joined hands with Hyder Ali on the promise of being gifted Wayanad. A large Coorg army camped in Wayanad to help Mysore troops. In 1776, Hyder Ali re-installed the Hindu Raja in Chirakkal and the latter joined Mysore's war effort to crush Pazhassi Raja. This triple alliance, which lasted till 1780, reached nowhere near defeating the Kottayam Army.

During his long war with Mysore and then the East India Company, Pazhassi Raja increased his sphere of influence significantly eastwards, as far as the outskirts of Mysore. His men regularly looted enemy treasuries and sandalwood from southern Karnataka while his enemies could do little to check these raids. This enabled him to lay claim on a great chunk of the Mysore district, as far as Nanjangod in the east. Also, Pazhassi Raja and his men frequently raided the domains of neighbouring Rajas in northern Malabar and Coorg to harass the enemy regiments posted there and he was often supported by the local population of those territories. Along with this, he had close ties with Ravi Varma and Krishna Varma, who were princes of Calicut and popular rebel leaders of southern Malabar.

T.H. Baber went to Mysore to direct operations himself and began a large search for informants and traitors. The East India Company itself admitted that they did not get a lot of informants as locals were devoted to the Raja, but some of those few informants proved devastating to revolt – one of them, a Chetti, found out where Raja had camped and informed Baber, who took to field with 100 Kolkars and 50 Sepoys.

There is one school of thought that blames Pazhayamviden Chandu as solely responsible for fall of Raja and end of his revolt. Pazhayamviden worked with the East India Company administration as an 'adviser' like Pallore Eman, but in reality, spied for the Raja. But in autumn of 1805, Pazhayamviden decided to betray all military secrets of his master for a large sum of money.

In the light of the above points, it will not be far-fetched to believe that Chetti, who guided the Company troops to Raja's hideout, mentioned by Baber in his letter, could be a servant or agent of Pazhayamviden Chandu.

On 30 November, 1805, Raja and his retainers were camped close to Karnataka on the shore of a stream, named Mavila or Mavila Tod [not far from Pulpally]. Raja and his party were caught by surprise and an intense but short fight followed. Six rebels were killed. One of the earliest rebels to be killed was Pazhassi Raja.

But evidently, the wounded Raja did live long enough for a few more minutes to raise his loaded gun and tell Canara Menon, an East India Company minor official, not to come too close to his dying body and pollute it. Raja's contempt and sarcasm for a man who chose to serve unclean foreigners was evident, but it also showed his uncompromising stand towards collaborators and foreign invaders.

The precise nature of Raja's death is controversial. Folklore insists that he committed suicide by swallowing a diamond ring to avoid capture after he was wounded but Baber says he was killed by a clerk named Canara Menon. W.J. Wilson, who wrote on the history of the Madras Regiment, credits Captain Clafam and his six sepoys for killing him. This third version is more likely as Baber was not on good terms with military authorities throughout the war. He is alleged to have credited Menon so as to deny credit to Clafam and his superior Colonel Hill.

Kunjani, the wife of Raja who was taken prisoner, committed suicide in captivity at Kappanaveedu, near Thalassery. As reprisal on his family, his property was confiscated and the palace at Pazhassi was demolished and replaced with a highway. The sorry state of his family aroused sympathy among the local Thiyyas, who were loyal followers and built a new house for his family.

□

53

Peer Ali Khan

(1812 – 7 July, 1857)

Peer Ali Khan was an Indian revolutionary and rebel, who participated in the Indian Independence movement. He was given capital punishment for participating in the freedom struggle of 1857.

Khan was a bookbinder by profession and he used to secretly distribute important leaflets, pamphlets and coded messages to freedom fighters. He conducted regular campaigns against the British Government.

He was arrested along with his 33 followers on 4 July, 1857.

On 7 July, 1857, Khan was hanged in full public view by William Tayler, the then Commissioner of Patna, along with 14 other rebels, including Ghasita Khalifa, Ghulam Abbas, Nandu Lal alias Sipahi, Jumman, Maduwa, Kajil Khan, Ramzani, Peer Bakhsh, Peer Ali, Wahid Ali, Ghulam Ali, Mahmood Akbar and Asrar Ali Khan.

□

54

P. Gopinathan Nair

(7 July, 1922 – 5 July, 2022)

P. Gopinathan Nair was an Indian social worker, Gandhian, independence activist, and the chairman of Mahatma Gandhi National Memorial Trust. He participated in the Quit India movement of 1942 and worked alongside Vinoba Bhave to promote Bhoodan and Gramdan movements. He was the initiator of the camp movement, a student program that was part of the Construction Movement of Mahatma Gandhi.

Gopinathan Nair was born on 7 July, 1922 to M. Padmanabha Pillai and K.P. Janaki Amma in Neyyattinkara, a town in the southern part of Thiruvananthapuram district of the south Indian state of Kerala. After completing his school education at the Government High School, Neyyattinkara, he did his university studies in science at the University College, Thiruvananthapuram.

During university, Nair participated in the Quit India movement. In 1944, he founded the Trivandrum Students Settlement movement with 35 students, inspired by the

Construction Movement of Mahatma Gandhi. In 1946, he became the Chief Tattwa Pracharak of the Kerala Gandhi Smarak Nidhi and conducted several courses for his colleagues as well as other students. During that same year, he completed further studies in Chinese culture and Gandhian philosophy at Shantiniketan.

For the next decade and a half, he set up camps for training people and carried out construction projects such as roads and sanitation facilities. He organised people for Bhoodan and Gramdan activities. When Vinoba Bhave visited Kerala as a part of his *Padayatra*, Nair organised a meeting in Kalady. Nair also became associated with Shanti Sena and was involved in many of its activities. He was reported to have been a mediator during the Naxalite insurgency in Kilimanoor in 1970, the Hindu-Muslim communal riots in Thalassery, the East Bengali refugee crisis of 1971, and the Kuttanad Peace Project of 1971 to 1976. He also served as the chair of the Sarva Seva Sangh in 1989 and was the convenor of the Cow Protection Committee in Kerala when Bhave campaigned against slaughter of cows. In the aftermath of the Marad massacre of 2002, Chief Minister A.K. Antony requested Nair's assistance in mediating between the warring factions; Nair was reportedly successful in his efforts.

Nair, who wrote several articles on Gandhian thought, was associated with Gandhi Smarak Nidhi in various positions. He held the post of the secretary of the Kerala chapter from 1980 to 1982, then became head of the chapter in 1999. He was elected as the national president of Gandhi Smarak Nidhi in 2012. In addition, Nair was a life member and a member of the governing board of the Gandhi Peace Foundation and president of the All India Sarva Seva Sangham, Varanasi (6 years) and Sevagram, Wardha (11 years). He was the chairman and patron of the Noorul Islam Civil Service Academy and a member of Sree Uthradam Thirunal Institute of Culture, Thiruvananthapuram.

Nair was married to L. Saraswathi Amma, a retired State Women's Welfare officer, and the couple lived in Neyyattinkara. Nair died from a heart attack at a private hospital in Neyyattinkara on 5 July, 2022, two days before his 100th birthday. He suffered from post-COVID-19 health complications and age-related ailments prior to his death.

□

55

Potti Sreeramulu

(16 March, 1901 – 15 December, 1952)

Potti Sreeramulu was an Indian revolutionary, revered as Amarajeevi ('immortal being') in the Andhra region for his self-sacrifice to the Andhra cause. Sreeramulu took part in the Indian Independence movement and was imprisoned for participating in the 1930 Salt Satyagraha. Between 1941 and 1942, he participated in the individual *satyagraha* and the Quit India movement, for which he was imprisoned on three occasions. He spent his life working for the Dalit community and other humanitarian work. He died during the hunger strike for 56 days in support of the formation of the Indian state for the Telugu-speaking population of Madras Presidency. He was involved in the village reconstruction programmes at Rajkot in Gujarat and Komaravolu in Krishna district of Andhra Pradesh. He joined the Gandhi Ashram established by Yerneni Subrahmanyam in Komaravolu. Commenting on Sreeramulu's dedication and fasting ability, Mahatma

Gandhi once said, "If only I have eleven more followers like Sreeramulu, I will win freedom from British rule in a year."

Between 1943 and 1944, he worked for the widespread adoption of *charkha* for textile-spinning in Nellore district. He was known for taking food provided by the households, regardless of caste or creed. He undertook three fasts, during 1946-1948, in support of the right of Dalits (a heterogenous group of oppressed Hindu caste, then referred to by Gandhi and his supporters by the contentious, though well-intentioned, term 'Harijan') to enter holy places, such as the temples of Vellore. He fasted in support of Dalit entry rights to the Venu Gopalaswamy temple in Moolapeta, Nellore – rights which were eventually secured. He again fasted to receive favourable orders, passed by the Madras government, to further uplift the Dalit community.

In an effort to protect the interests of the Telugu people of Madras Presidency and to preserve the culture of Andhra people, he attempted to force the government to listen to the public demand for the separation of the Andhra region from Madras Presidency, based on linguistic lines and with Madras as its capital. He went on a lengthy fast, stopping when Prime Minister Jawaharlal Nehru promised to support the creation of Andhra state. Despite this concession, little progress was made on the issue, largely due to the Telugu people's insistence on retention of Madras as their future capital. The JVP (Jawahar, Vallabhbhai, Pattabhi) Committee, headed by Jawaharlal Nehru, Vallabhbhai Patel and Pattabhi Sitaramayya, would not accept that proposal.

With the Andhra state still not granted, Sreeramulu

resumed his hunger strike at the Madras house of Maharshi Bulusu Sambamurti on 19 October, 1952, despite the entreaties of his supporters who stated that retention of Madras was a futile cause. Despite the Andhra Congress Committee's disavowal of the fast, this action captured the public attention.

Despite strikes and demonstrations by the Andhra people, the government made no clear statement regarding the formation of the new state, and Sreeramulu died on the night of 15 December, 1952.

In his death procession, people shouted slogans praising his sacrifice, with thousands more joining in, as the procession reached Mount Road, Madras. The procession broke into a riot and accompanying destruction of public property. As the news spread, disorder broke out in Vizianagaram, Visakhapatnam, Vijayawada, Bhimavaram, Tadepalligudem, Rajahmundry, Eluru, Guntur, Tenali, Ongole, Kanigiri and Nellore. Police fatally shot down seven people in Anakapalle and Vijayawada. The popular agitation continued for three to four days, disrupting normal life in Madras and Andhra regions. On 19 December, 1952, Prime Minister Nehru announced that a separate Andhra state would be formed.

□

56

Pratap Singh Barhat

(24 May 1893 – 7 May 1918)

Pratap Singh Barhat was an activist in the freedom strugglel from Rajasthan. He took a prominent part in the revolutionary movement against British rule in India. He was the son of Kesari Singh Barhat.

Born on 24 May, 1893 at Udaipur, in Udaipur district of the Indian state of Rajasthan, he joined the Revolutionary Party as a follower of Rash Behari Bose. He participated in the revolutionary plot to throw a bomb at Lord Hardinge, Viceroy of India on 3 December, 1912. His uncle Jorawar Singh Barhat was also in that group. He was arrested in the Benaras Conspiracy Case and was sentenced in February 1916 to five years of RI. He was subjected to brutal torture in Bareilly Central Jail to force him to divulge the names of his compatriots. He refused. He died in the jail on 24 May, 1918 as an unsung hero.

□

57

Prithvi Singh Azad

(15 September, 1892 – 5 March, 1989)

Prithvi Singh Azad was an Indian Independence activist, revolutionary and one of the founder members of Ghadar Party. He suffered incarceration several times during the pre-Independence period, including a term in the Cellular Jail. The Government of India awarded him the third highest civilian honour of the Padma Bhushan, in 1977, for his contributions to society. Prithvi Singh Azad was born on 15 September, 1892 at Lalru, a small town in Mohali district of Punjab. He was a Rajput, but he did a lot of work for the upliftment of Dalits. He was attracted to the nationalist movement while he was still in his teens and was reported to have been influenced by the arrest of Lokmanya Tilak and Khudiram Bose by the British government in 1907-08. He visited the US in 1912 and it was during this time that he met Lala Har Dayal, one of the founders of later-day Ghadar Party, a militant organisation formed by Indians in North America for the

liberation of India. He also assisted in the establishment of *Hindustan Ghadar*, the mouthpiece of the party. Returning to India, along with around 150 freedom fighters, he was captured by the British on 7 December, 1914, tried, sentenced to 10 years' imprisonment and spent time in various jails, including Calcutta, Madras and the Cellular Jail. After the initial futile attempt, he escaped by jumping out of a running train while he was being transferred from one jail to another. Later, he became an associate of Chandrashekhar Azad and reportedly received a Mauser pistol from him. [citation needed] It was reported that Azad was with Chandrashekhar Azad just before the British forces surrounded him at Alfred Park on 27 February, 1931, but the latter asked Prithvi Singh to escape while deciding to continue his battle with the forces; alternatively, another contention was that the two Azads met at Alfred Park a few days before the death of Chandrashekhar.

It was Chandrashekhar who advised Azad to visit Russia for further training; it was reported that the idea to send Azad to Russia in fact came from Bhagat Singh, another martyred revolutionary and Chandrashekhar conveyed Bhagat Singh's request. He visited Russia to spend a few months there and his experiences in Russia were later published as a book, *Lenin ke Desham Mein*, which was subsequently translated into English by Vijay Chauhan under the title, *Prithvi Singh Azad in Lenin's Land*. On his return to India, he met several mainstream freedom fighters, including Mohandas Gandhi and joined the nationalist movement led by Gandhi. Between 1933 and India's Independence in 1947, he was arrested several times and one of which included the Lahore

Conspiracy Case in which he was sentenced to death; the sentence was later commuted to life imprisonment in the Cellular Jail.

After India's Independence, he successfully contested the elections to the first Constituent Assembly of India from Punjab and was its member since the assembly met for the first time at Constitution Club Hall, New Delhi on 9 December, 1946. After the Indian Independence, he was selected as the Minister for Labour and Local Self-government, the only Harijan member of the ministry, when Bhim Sen Sachar took over as the second Chief Minister of Punjab, in 1949. The Government of India honoured him with the civilian honor of Padma Bhushan in 1977.

Azad died on 5 March, 1989, at the age of 96. The story of his life has been documented in two autobiographies; *Kranti Path ka Pathik* (A Traveller on the Revolutionary Path), which was published in 1990 by Haryana Sahitya Akademi while *Baba Prithvi Singh Azad* (*The Legendary Crusader*) was published by Bharatiya Vidya Bhavan three years earlier, in 1987. A set of documents related to his life have been preserved in the Nehru Memorial Museum and Library, New Delhi as 'Baba Prithvi Singh Azad Papers'. A local hospital in Lalru, his native place, is being considered for renaming as Baba Prithvi Singh Azad Memorial Hospital. His daughter, Pragya Kumar, is a medical doctor and the Chief Medical Officer at Punjab University, Chandigarh.

□

58

Rao Gopal Singh Kharwa

(1872–1939)

Rao Gopal Singh Kharwa, born in Rajasthan, was the ruler of the Kharwa state (near Ajmer) of Rajputana. He was sentenced to four years' imprisonment in the Todgarh Fort, located approximately 70 kms (43 miles) from Beawar for organising a revolt against the British. He was president of Akhil Bharatiya Kshatriya Mahasabha for the year 1924. In 1989, India's Postal Department issued a postage stamp depicting his picture in his honour. Every spring on the anniversary of his death, the residents of Kharwa and nearby villages gather at a *mela* (celebration or fair) to commemorate their former Thakur. He was a Rathore Rajput by birth and believed in upholding the duties of a Rajput ruler towards his people at all costs.

□

59

Rati Ram Deshbandhu Gupta

(14 June, 1901 – 21 November, 1951)

Rati Ram Deshbandhu Gupta, more popularly known as Lala Deshbandhu Gupta, was an Indian freedom fighter, legislator and journalist, born in Panipat, Haryana to Shri Shadiram and Rajrani Gupta. He is widely known for championing the freedom of the press and for arguing for assembly status for the national capital territory of Delhi. He also argued for the separation of Punjab and Haryana. Deshbandhu Gupta was born as Rati Ram Gupta in the Badi Pahad area of Panipat. His father Shadiram was a petition-writer and a Vedic scholar. He also wrote Urdu prose and poetry. He was nineteen years old when he married the 17-year old Sona Devi, though their matrimonial alliance had been arranged since he was five-years old and she was three. He had four sons: Vishwabandhu Gupta, Prembandhu Gupta, Ramesh Gupta and Satish Gupta.

Rati Ram Gupta completed his elementary education at a *madrasa* in Panipat, and then studied at St Stephen's

College. Charles Indridge Western and Ghosh taught him there, while S.K. Rudra was the principal. He also worked as assistant for Shri Jamnalal Bajaj, a cloth merchant at Chandini Chowk for 18 days, when he was at St Stephen's College.

It was around this time that events, such as the Jallianwalla Bagh massacre took place. They left their imprint on public memory at large and on the young Rati Ram in particular. As a result, following a Non-Cooperation Conference by Mahatma Gandhi in Bhiwani on 22 October, 1920, Deshbandhu Gupta was inspired to play a more direct role in the struggle for freedom against British rule in India. He gave the principal of the college, S.K. Rudra, a notice to the effect that he wished to leave St Stephen's. As S.K. Rudra was sympathetic to the revolutionary cause, he accepted this and is noted to have encouraged the young Rati Ram to make the best of his decision to serve the freedom struggle.

Deshbandhu Gupta's active involvement in political events of his time was a major factor in his inclusion in important events associated with the Indian freedom struggle. He displayed social awareness and an interest in being part of important administration with organisations he was familiar with even before joining the INC. For example, he was an active member of the Arya Samaj branch at Chawri Bazar. He also came to hold the post of councillor of the branch at one point of time. He suffered political incarceration on a number of occasions as a result of his active involvement in the freedom struggle. He was first imprisoned at the age of nineteen.

He is known to have campaigned for the separation

of Haryana and Punjab upon release from jail in 1927. He was supported by Ch. Ranbir Huda in this, possibly among others.

Among other members of the freedom movement, he was associated with both Lala Lajpat Rai and Swami Shraddhananda. The former was his teacher at the Tilak School of Politics. He later became the confidante of Lala Lajpat Rai.

He once addressed a gathering in Delhi at the behest of the women's wing of the INC. As the content of his speech was considered objectionable by the British Government, he was banned from addressing any other gathering in Delhi. As a result, Lajpat Rai assigned him the task of organising Congress Committees at Karnal, which was the *tehsil* of his birthplace Panipat.

The Government of India Act 1935 was passed as a result of deliberations in the Third Round Table Conference in London that was convened in November 1932. It provided for the setting up of an All India Federation and new governance models for the provinces. There were several shortcomings in the Act, the thrust of which was that, though Indians could have greater provincial administrative power, the key departments – defence and foreign relations – were still the prerogative of the British. Despite being 'bitterly opposed' to the provisions of the Act, the INC went ahead with elections and formed governments in seven out of eleven provinces by July 1937, and coalition governments in two more later on. It was only Bengal and Punjab that had non-Congress governments. Punjab was ruled by the Unionist Party and Bengal by the Krishak Praja Party-Muslim League coalition. On February 18 Legislative

Assembly elections in Punjab, only Lala Deshbandhu Gupta and Pandit Shriram Sharma won seats from the INC. He stayed on in the Punjab Assembly for seven years. He was later elected MP from Delhi and also held several important positions within the INC during his political career. It was Swami Shraddhananda and Mahatma Gandhi who gave him the title 'Deshbandhu' (friend of the nation), which came to be used as his name.

In addition to active politics, he was involved in countering the many communal riots witnessed in Delhi and at many other areas in British India during this time as an outcome of growing communally-divisive forces in Indian society.

As both a journalist and Constituent Assembly member, he is known to have staunchly supported freedom of the Press in India, as especially evidenced in the debates surrounding the (then) entry 88-A in the Assembly draft, held in September 1949.

Yet another major issue he is known to have been involved with is the question of Assembly status for the national capital, Delhi. He supported the setting up of a responsible government in Delhi, which led him to oppose B.R. Ambedkar on the issue. Dr.Ambedkar supported special status for the NCT. Delhi eventually did get an Assembly, though as a special Union Territory rather than a state. It is for his role in securing this that Deshbandhu Gupta is believed to have been a likely candidate for the first Chief Minister of Delhi.

□

60

Sagarmal Gopa

(3 November, 1900 – 4 April, 1946)

Sagarmal Gopa was a freedom fighter and patriot from Rajasthan. His father is Akhairaj Gopa. He took active part in the non-co-operation movement in 1921. He opposed anti-people policies of the rulers of Jaisalmer. He was expelled from Jaisalmer and Hyderabad. Even in exile, he continued to work for the freedom movement. After his father's death in 1941, on his return to Jaisalmer, he was arrested on 25 May, 1941. He was tortured in prison for years. He was burnt to death in the prison on 4 April, 1946. Three books written by Gopa are: (1) Aazadi ke Diwane, (2) Jaisalmer ka Gundaraj (3) Raghunath Singh ka Mukadma. The Government of India issued a postage stamp in 1986 in honour of Sagarmal Gopa. A branch of Indira Gandhi Canal is named after him.

□

61

Sangolli Rayanna

(15 August, 1796 – 26 January, 1831)

Sangolli Rayanna was an Indian revolutionary, military chief (*shetsanadi*) and warrior in the Kittur princely state of present-day state of Karnataka. He was the *shetsanadi* of the kingdom of Kittur ruled at the time by Rani Chennamma and fought the British East India Company till his death. His life was the subject of the 2012 Kannada film, 'Sangolli Rayanna'. He belonged to the Kuruba family.

Sangolli Rayanna participated in the 1824 rebellion and was arrested by the British, who released him later. He continued to fight the British and wanted to instal the adopted son of King Mallasarja and Rani Chennamma, namely Shivalingappa, as the ruler of Kittur. He mobilised the local people and started a guerilla type of warfare against the British. He and his guerrilla army moved from place to place, burnt government offices, waylaid British troops and plundered treasuries. Most of his land was confiscated and what remained of it was heavily taxed. He taxed the landlords and built up an army from among the common people. The British troops could not defeat him in an open battle. Hence, by treachery, he was caught in April 1830 and tied up by the British; he was sentenced to death. Shivalingappa, the boy who was supposed to be the new ruler, was also arrested by the British. Rayanna was helped by Gajaveera, a Siddi warrior, in his revolt against the British in 1829-30.

Rayanna was executed by hanging from a banyan tree, about 4 kilometers from Nandagad in Belagavi district on 26 January, 1831. He was buried near Nandagad. Legend says that a close associate, Sangolli Bichugatti Channabasappa of Rayanna, planted a banyan sapling on his grave. The tree is fully grown and stands to this day. An Ashoka *stambha* was installed near the tree. A small temple in the name of Sangolli Rayanna was constructed at Sangolli village, in which stands a statue of Rayanna flanked by two wooden weights used for body building. Two wooden weights are original and are supposed to have been used by Rayanna himself for body building. A community hall built in commemoration of Rayanna at Sangolli serves the villagers. The Karnataka government recently established the Krantiveera Sangolli Rayanna Authority which is engaged in establishing the Kantiveera Sangolli Rayanna Sainik School, 'Shouryabhoomi' Krantiveera Sangolli Rayanna rock garden and a Veerabhoomi Krantiveer Sangolli Rayanna museum.

□

62

Shambhu Dutt Sharma

(9 September, 1918 – 15 April, 2016)

Shambhu Dutt Sharma was an Indian Gandhian, freedom fighter and anti-corruption activist. He joined Mahatma Gandhi's Quit India movement in 1942, at the age of 24, after resigning as a civilian gazetted officer in the British Indian Army. Shambhu Dutt was a law graduate. He was imprisoned.

In 1975 he was again imprisoned for protesting during the Emergency in India imposed by Prime Minister Indira Gandhi.

In 2007, when serving as the honorary general secretary of the Gandhian Satyagraha Brigade, Sharma said, "Corruption has become rampant. It has to be wiped out. On this issue we will start the *satyagraha*." He favoured the adoption of the Corrupt Public Servants (Forfeiture of Property) Bill prepared by the Law Commission of India in 1999, which proposed to bar criminals from contesting elections.

At the age of 92 on 15 April, 2016, he ended his fast

unto death, demanding the end of corruption in India, persuaded by several prominent people, including Kiran Bedi, Swami Agnivesh and also by Prashant Bhushan. However, he felt betrayed because Anna Hazare was getting media attention.

He was also the founder of Transparency International India. Sharma's team was known as Gandhian Seva Brigade.

□

63

Shyamji Krishna Varma

(4 October, 1857 – 30 March, 1930)

Shyamji Krishna Varma was an Indian revolutionary fighter, an Indian patriot, lawyer and journalist who founded the Indian Home Rule Society, India House and *The Indian Sociologist* in London. A graduate of Balliol College, Krishna Varma was a noted scholar in Sanskrit and other Indian languages. He pursued a brief legal career in India and served as the Diwan in a number of Indian princely states. He had, however, differences with Crown authorities, was dismissed following a supposed conspiracy by local British officials at Junagadh and chose to return to England. An admirer of Dayanand Saraswati's approach to cultural nationalism and of Herbert Spencer, Krishna Varma believed in Spencer's dictum: 'Resistance to aggression is not simply justified, but imperative'.

In 1905, he founded the India House and *The Indian Sociologist*, which rapidly developed as an organised meeting point for radical nationalists among Indian students in Britain at the time and one of the most prominent centres for revolutionary Indian nationalism outside India. Krishna Varma moved to Paris in 1907, to avoid prosecution.

In 1905, Shyamji focused his activity as a political propagandist and organiser for the complete Independence of India. Shyamji made his debut in Indian politics by publishing the first issue of his English monthly, *The Indian Sociologist*, an organ and of political, social and religious reforms. This was an assertive, ideological monthly aimed at inspiring mass opposition to British rule, which stimulated many intellectuals to fight for Independence of India.

On 18 February, 1905, Shyamji inaugurated a new organiszation, called The Indian Home Rule Society. The first meeting, held at his Highgate home, unanimously decided to found The Indian Home Rule Society with the object of securing Hhome Rrule for India.

1. Carrying on propaganda in England by all practical means with a view to attain the same.
2. Spreading among the people of India the objectives of freedom and national unity.

Death and Commemoration

Shyamji published two more issues of *Indian Sociologist* in August and September 1922, before ill health prevented him from continuing. He died in hospital at 11:30 p.m. on 30 March, 1930, leaving behind his wife, Bhanumati Krishna Varma. News of his death was suppressed by the British Government in India. Nevertheless, tributes were paid to him by Bhagat Singh and other inmates at Lahore Jail where they were undergoing a long-term drawn-out trial. *Maratha*, an English daily newspaper started by Bal

Gangadhar Tilak, paid tribute to him. He had made prepaid arrangements with the local government of Geneva and St. Georges cemetery to preserve his and his wife's ashes at the cemetery for 100 years and to send their urns to India, whenever it became independent during that period. Requested by Paris-based scholar Dr Prithwindra Mukherjee, the then Prime Minister Indira Gandhi agreed to repatriate the ashes. Finally on 22 August, 2003, the urns of ashes of Shyamji and his wife Bhanumati were handed over to then Chief Minister of Gujarat state, Narendra Modi by the Ville de Genève and the Swiss government, 55 years after India's Independence. They were brought to Mumbai and after a long procession throughout Gujarat, they reached Mandvi, his birthplace. A memorial, called Kranti Teerth dedicated to him, was built and inaugurated in 2010, near Mandvi. Spread over 52 acres, the memorial complex houses a replica of India House building at Highgate along with statues of Shyamji Krishna Varma and his wife. Urns containing Krishna Varma's ashes, those of his wife, and a gallery dedicated to earlier activists of Indian Independence movement are housed within the memorial. Krishna Verma was disbarred from the Inner Temple in 1909. This decision was revisited in 2015, and a unanimous decision was taken to posthumously reinstate him. In the 1970s, a new town, developed in his native state of Kutch, was named after him as Shyamji Krishna Varmanagar in his memory and honour.

India Post released postal stamps and first day covers commemorating him. Kutch University was renamed after him. The India Post issued a postal stamp on Shyamji Krishna Varma on 4 October, 1989.

□

64

Sucheta Mazumdar

(25 June, 1908 – 1 December, 1974)

Sucheta Mazumdar (married name, Sucheta Kripalani) was an Indian freedom fighter. She was born in Ambala, Punjab (now in Haryana) into a Bengali Brahmo Samaj family. Her father Surendranath Majumdar worked as a medical officer, a job that required many transfers. As a result, she attended a number of schools, her final degree being a Master's in History from St. Stephen's College, Delhi. This was a time when the country's atmosphere was charged with nationalist sentiments and the freedom struggle was gaining momentum. She was not born with a steely will and exemplary leadership qualities. Rather, she was a shy child, self-conscious about her appearance and intellect, as she points out in her book, *An Unfinished Autobiography*. It was the age she grew up in and the situations she faced that shaped her personality. Sucheta recounts how, as a ten-year old, she and her siblings had heard their father and his friends talk about the Jallianwala Bagh massacre. It left

them so outraged that they vented their anger on some of the Anglo-Indian children they played with, by calling them names.

Her exact words were, "I could understand enough to feel great anger against the British, after hearing about the Jallianwala Bagh massacre. I and my sister Sulekha vented out anger on some of the Anglo-Indian children who played with us, calling them all kinds of names." Both Sucheta and her sister Sulekha were desperate to join India's burgeoning Independence movement. There is one particularly fascinating incident which Sucheta narrates in her book. After the Jallianwala Bagh massacre, the Prince of Wales visited Delhi. Girls from her school were taken to stand near the Kudsia Garden to honour the Prince of Wales. Despite wanting to refuse, both the sisters couldn't and that left them bitterly outraged at their apparent cowardice.

Like her contemporaries Aruna Asaf Ali and Usha Mehta, she came to the forefront during the Quit India movement and was arrested by the British. She later worked closely with Mahatma Gandhi during the Partition riots. She accompanied him to Noakhali in 1946. Mahatma Gandhi describe her as "a person of rare courage and character who brought credit to Indian womanhood." She was one of the few women who were elected to the Constituent Assembly of India. She was elected as the first woman Chief Minister of Uttar Pradesh state from the Kanpur constituency and was part of the subcommittee that drafted the Indian Constitution. She became a part of the subcommittee that laid down the charter for the constitution of India. On 14 August, 1947, she sang 'Vande Mataram' in the Independence session of the Constituent Assembly a few minutes before Nehru delivered his famous 'Tryst with Destiny' speech. She was also the founder of the All India Mahila Congress, established in 1940. After Independence, she remained involved with politics. For the first Lok Sabha elections in 1952, she contested from New Delhi on a KMPP ticket. She had joined the short-lived party founded by her husband the year before. She defeated the Congress candidate Manmohini Sehgal. Five years later, she was re-elected from the same constituency, but this time as the Congress candidate. She was elected one last time to the Lok Sabha in 1967, from Gonda constituency of Uttar Pradesh.

Meanwhile, she had also become a member of the Uttar Pradesh Legislative Assembly. From 1960 to 1963, she served as Minister of Labour, Community Development and Industry in the Uttar Pradesh government. In October 1963, she became the Chief Minister of Uttar Pradesh, the first woman to hold that position in any Indian state. The highlight of her tenure was the firm handling of a state employees' strike. This first-ever strike by the state employees continued for sixty-two days. She relented only when the employees' leaders agreed to compromise. Kripalani kept her reputation as a firm administrator by refusing their demand for a pay hike.

When the Congress split in 1969, she left the party with Morarji Desai faction to form NCO. She lost the 1971 election as the NCO candidate from Faizabad (Lok Sabha constituency). She retired from politics in 1971 and remained in seclusion, till her death in 1974.

□

65

Swami Keshwanandd

(12 March, 1883 – 13 September, 1972)

Swami Keshwanand was born in a Jat family of Magloona village in Sikar district of present-day Rajasthan, in 1883. Swamiji, whose actual name was Birama, was the son of Thakarsi, a penurious camel-driver and his wife Saran. The family were Hindu and belonged to the Dhaka gotra and the Jat clan.

When Birama was five, his family left Magluna for the nearby town of Ratangarh.Thakarsi, where he used to escort prosperous Seths (businessman) from Ratangarh to Delhi on his camel. He died in 1890 when Birama was seven. This put paid to Birama's already slim chances of gaining an education. It is said that for a prolonged period, his mother had perforce to move from place to place in search of shelter and fodder for her animals. Mother and son finally settled down at village Kelania, in present-day Sri Ganganagar district, in 1897. However, this was not the end of their misfortunes: Rajasthan was then headed towards one of its periodic famines. By one account: "There was no vegetation left on the ground. There was no drop of water. All the animals died for want of fodder. People survived on grasses and the bark of 'Khejri' trees. Even that also became scarce. There was nothing like governance. The ruling *samants* were least bothered about the poor people..." It was in these circumstances that Birama's mother Saran died in 1899, at village Kelania.

The Jalianwalla Bagh massacre of 1919, which cast a profound impact on the collective psyche of Punjab, left Swami Keshawanand profoundly moved. He started attending the meetings of the Indian National Congress, joined the Indian Independence movement under the leadership of Mahatma Gandhi and participated in the non-co-operation movement, for which he was imprisoned for two years (1921-1922) at Ferozepur. In 1930, he was given charge of Congress activities in Ferozepur district. He was again arrested the same year, but was soon released pursuant to the Gandhi-Irwin Pact.

Swami Keshwanand's deep understanding of the rural society of the desert region can be gleaned from his book, *Maru Bhumi Seva Karya*. In this book, he has explained the peculiarities of the desert region, identified the problems and suggested solutions. It was Swami Keshwanand's lifelong endeavour to eradicate social evils, like untouchability, illiteracy, child marriage, indebtedness, poverty, backwardness, alcohol abuse, moral dissipation, etc.

Swami Keshwanand, born in a Jat Hindu family of Dhaka clan, and a renunciate belonging to the Udasi sect, which was propagated by Srichandji, son of guru Nanakdev, the founder of Sikh faith, was a unique example of communal harmony. He organised celebrations in honour of Sikh, Bishnoi, Namdhari and Jain *gurus*. During the Partition of India in 1947, he got wounded Muslims admitted him to hospitals and arranged food and shelter for them. Swami Keshwanand started a girls' school, called GramothanVidyapeath at Sangriya, in August 1917. Because of his efforts, many others in Sangriya have prioritised education.

Swami Keshwanand was presented the 'Abhinandan Granth' by the then Chief Minister of Rajasthan, on 9 March, 1958. He was a member of the Rajya Sabha for two consecutive terms, 1952-58 and 1958-64. He died on 13 September, 1972 at Delhi. The Department of Posts, Government of India, issued a commemorative postage stamp in his honour on 15 August, 1999. In 2009, Swami Keshwanand Rajasthan Agricultural University was named after him.

□

66

Tarak Nath Das

(15 June, 1884 – 22 December, 1958)

Tarak Nath Das was an Indian revolutionary and internationalist scholar. He was a pioneering immigrant in the west coast of North America and discussed his plans with Tolstoy, while organising the Asian Indian immigrants in favour of the Indian Independence movement. He was a professor of Political Science at Columbia University and a visiting faculty in several other universities. 'A direct appeal to the Sikhs' appeared in the September-October 1909 issue of the *Free Hindustan*, reproduced by the *Swadesh Sevak*; the article ended with: "Coming in contact with free people and institutions of free nations, some of the Sikhs, though labourers in the North American continent, have assimilated the idea of liberty and trampled the medals of slavery..."

In March 1912, a letter published in *The Punjabee*, asked for a leader to come and help organise Indians in the area in view of the rising revolutionary spirit.

Originally they discussed inviting Kumar and then Sardar Ajit Singh. However, when Tarak arrived, he suggested inviting Lala Hardayal, whom he knew from his days at Stanford University. Hardayal agreed to work with him, setting up the Hindi Association of the Pacific Ocean, which provided the first basis for the Ghadar Party. "Many of the leaders were of other parties and from different parts of India, Hardayal, Ras Bihari Bose, Barakatulah, Seth Husain Rahim, Tarak Nath Das and Vishnu Ganesh Pingley. The Ghadar was the first organised violent bid for freedom after the rising of 1857. Many hundreds paid the price with their lives," wrote Khushwant Singh.

Tarak was among those who suffered emotionally from the Partition of India in 1947 and vehemently opposed the process of balkanisation of South Asia till his last day. After forty-six years in exile, he revisited his motherland in 1952, as a Visiting Professor of the Watumull Foundation. He founded the Vivekananda Society in Calcutta. On 9 September, 1952, he presided over the public meeting to celebrate the 37th anniversary of Bagha Jatin's heroic martyrdom, urging the youth to revive the values upheld by his mentor, Jatindâ. He died upon return to the United States on 22 December, 1958, aged 74.

□

67

Tara Rani Srivastava

(1675 – 1761)

Tara Rani Srivastava was an Indian freedom fighter and part of Mahatma Gandhi's Quit India movement. She and her husband, Phulendu Babu, lived in the Saran district of Bihar. In 1942, she and her husband were leading a march in Siwan towards the police station, when the husband was shot dead by the police. She nonetheless continued the march, returning later to find that her husband had died. She remained part of the struggle for freedom until the country's Independence five years later.

On 12 August, 1942, when called upon by Mahatma Gandhi, she and her husband organised a march to raise the flag of India in front of the Siwan police station – an act that would be seen as "a major defiance". The police, in preventing them from hoisting the flag, *lathi*-charged the protesters. When they were unable to gain control, the

police opened fire. Phulendu Babu was among the shot and wounded. Despite that, after bandaging Babu's wounds with strips of cloth torn from her sari, Tara Rani continued her march to the police station, where she attempted to hoist the flag. On her return, she discovered that her husband had died of his injuries. On 15 August, 1942, a prayer meeting was held in Chhapra in honour of her husband's sacrifice for the country. She continued to be part of the freedom struggle until the Partition of India on 15 August, 1947.

□

68

Thacheril Govindan Kutty Menon

(2 March, 1940 – 12 June, 2021)

Thacheril Govindan Kutty Menon is an Indian social worker and environmentalist. His contributions are reported in the introduction of environmentally friendly irrigation and farming techniques under the aegis of Kasturbagram in Indore, Madhya Pradesh. He is known to have promoted biodynamic agriculture in India. He received the Jamnalal Bajaj Award in 1989. The Government of India awarded him the fourth highest civilian honour of the Padma Shri in 1991.

□

69

Tirot Sing

(1802 – 17 July, 1835)

Tirot Sing, also known as U Tirot Sing Syiem, was born in the year 1802 and died in the year 1835. He was one of the chiefs of the Khasi people in the early 19th century. He drew his lineage from the Syiemlieh clan. He was *syiem* (chief) of Nongkhlaw, part of the Khasi Hills. His surname was Syiemlieh. He was a constitutional head, sharing corporate authority with his Council comprising general representatives of the leading clans within his territory. Tirot Sing declared war and fought against British for attempts to take over control of the Khasi Hills.

He died on 17 July, 1835. His death is commemorated in Meghalaya as U Tirot Sing Day. The British had gained control over the Brahmaputra valley after concluding the Treaty of Yandabo in 1826. Between their possessions in Sylhet and the newly acquired possessions in Lower Assam, lay the Khasi Hills. They wanted to construct a road through this area to connect Gauhati with Sylhet to save weeks of travel and malaria-inflicted country.

David Scott, the agent to the British Governor-General for the northern territory, found out that U Tirot Sing was interested in regaining possessions in the *duars* (passes into Assam) in return for the permission for the road project. After a two-day session of the *durbar* (court), the Assembly agreed to the proposal of the British. Work on the road started. When Balaram Singh, Raja of Ranee, disputed U Tirot Sing's claims to the *duars*, he went with a party of armed men in December 1828 to establish his claim. He was confident that the British would support him; instead, he was confronted by a party of sepoys who blocked his passage. When news came that the British were reinforcing forces in Assam, U Tirot Sing convened a *durbar* again and passed orders for the British to evacuate Nongkhlaw. The British did not pay any heed and the Khasis attacked the British garrison in Nongkhlaw on 4 April, 1829. His men killed two British officers, and thus unleashed the fury of British retaliation. Military operations against U Tirot Sing and other Khasi chiefs started immediately.

In the Anglo-Khasi war, the Khasis lacked firearms and had only swords, shields, bows and arrows. They were untrained in the British type of warfare and soon found that it was impossible to engage in open battle against an enemy who could kill from a distance. Therefore, they resorted to guerrilla activity, which dragged on for about four years.

Tirot Sing fought with native weapons, such as a sword and shield. He was shot at by the British and had to hide in a cave. He was eventually captured by the British in January 1833 and deported to Dacca. The location of his hiding place was given by a chief of his who was bribed with gold coins by the British. He died on 17 July, 1835. His death anniversary is commemorated every year as a state holiday in Meghalaya.

□

70

Tiruppur Kumaran

(4 October, 1904 – 11 January, 1932)

Kumaran, also known as Tiruppur Kumaran or Kodi Kaatha Kumaran, was an Indian revolutionary and freedom fighter, who participated in the Indian Independence movement. His parents were Nachimuthu and Karuppaayi. He founded the Desa Bandhu Youth Association and led protests against the British. He died due to injuries sustained from a police assault on the banks of Noyyal river in Tiruppur during a protest march against the British government on 11 January, 1932. At the time of his death, he was holding the flag of the Indian nationalists, which had been banned by the British, giving rise to the epithet 'Kodi kaatha Kumaran' in Tamil, which means 'Kumaran, who protected the flag'.

A commemorative stamp was issued by India post in October 2004 on his 100th birth anniversary. A statue has been erected in Tirupur in his honour and it often used as a focal point for public demonstrations.

□

71

Usha Mehta

(25 March, 1920 – 11 August, 2000)

Usha Mehta was a Gandhian and freedom fighter of India. She is also remembered for organizing the Congress Radio, also called the Secret Congress Radio, an underground radio station, which functioned for few months during the Quit India Movement of 1942. In 1998, the Government of India conferred on her Padma Vibhushan, the second highest civilian award of Republic of India.

Gandhi and the Congress had announced that the Quit India Movement would commence on 9 August 1942 with a rally at Gowalia Tank grounds in Mumbai. Nearly all leaders including Gandhi were arrested before that date. However, a vast crowd of Indians gathered at Gowalia Tank Ground on the appointed day. It was left to a group of junior leaders and workers to address them and hoist the national flag.

On 14 August 1942, Usha and some of her close associates began the Secret Congress Radio, a clandestine radio station. It went air on 27 August. The first words broadcast in her voice were: "This is the Congress radio calling on 42.34 metres from somewhere in India." Her associates included Vithalbhai Jhaveri, Chandrakant Jhaveri, Babubhai Thakkar and Nanka Motwani, owner of Chicago Radio, who supplied equipment and provided technicians. Many other leaders, including Dr. Ram Manohar Lohia, Achyutrao Patwardhan and Purushottam Trikamdas, also assisted the Secret Congress Radio. The radio broadcast recorded messages from Gandhi and other prominent leaders across India. To elude the authorities, the organizers moved the station's location almost daily. Ultimately, however, the police found them on 12 November 1942 and arrested the organizers, including Usha Mehta. All were later imprisoned.

The Criminal Investigation Department (CID), a wing of the Indian Police, interrogated her for six months. During this time, she was held in solitary confinement and offered inducements such as the opportunity to study abroad if she would betray the movement. However, she chose to remain silent and, during her trials, asked the Judge of the High Court whether she was required to answer the questions. When the judge confirmed that she was not mandatory, she declared that she would not reply to any of the questions, not even to save herself. After the trial, she was sentenced to four years' imprisonment (1942 to 1946). Two of her associates were also convicted. Usha was imprisoned at Yeravda Jail in Pune. Her health deteriorated and she was sent to Bombay for treatment at Sir J. J. Hospital. In the hospital, three to four policemen kept a round-the-clock watch on her to prevent her from escaping. When her health improved, she was returned to Yeravda Jail. In March 1946, she was released, the first political prisoner to be released in Bombay, at the orders of Morarji Desai, who was at that time the home minister in the interim government. Although the Secret Congress Radio functioned only for three months, it greatly assisted the movement by disseminating uncensored news and other information banned by the British-controlled government of India. Secret Congress Radio also kept the leaders of the freedom movement in touch with the public. Reminiscing about those days, Usha Mehta described her involvement with the Secret Congress Radio as her "finest moment" and also as her saddest moment, because an Indian technician had betrayed them to the authorities.

With time, Usha grew increasingly unhappy with the developments taking place in the social, political, and economic spheres of independent India. Once, in an interview to India Today, she expressed her feelings in these words: "Certainly this is not the freedom we fought for." She added that the freedom fighters of her generation felt that "once people were ensconced in positions of power, the rot would set in." However, in her words, "we didn't know the rot would sink in so soon." Nevertheless, she did not deny the achievements of free India since the independence: "India has survived as a democracy and even built a good industrial base," she said. "Still, it is not the India of our dreams".

In August 2000, although she was suffering from fever, Usha participated like she did every year in the anniversary celebrations related to the Quit India Movement in August Kranti Maidan. She returned home weak and exhausted. Two days later, she died peacefully on 11 August 2000 at the age of 80.

□

72

Uyyalawada Narasimha Reddy

(24 November, 1806 – 22 February, 1847)

Uyyalawada Narasimha Reddy was an Indian freedom fighter. Son of a farmer, Telugu Palegaadu Mallareddy and Seethamma, Narasimha Reddy was born in Rupanagudi village, on 24 November, 1806. He belonged to the Velanati clan of the Reddys. He and his commander-in-chief Vadde Obanna were at the heart of the rebellion against the British in 1847, where 5,000 peasants rose up against the British East India Company in Kurnool district. They were protesting against the changes introduced by the British in the traditional agrarian system during the first half of the nineteenth century. These changes included the introduction of the *ryotwari* system and other attempts to maximise revenue collection by exploiting the lower-status cultivators and by depleting their crops which left them impoverished. He killed over 3,000 British East India Company soldiers during the course of the revolt.

The East India Company's introduction in the

Chennai Presidency of the 1803 Permanent Settlement, which had first been enacted in Bengal Presidency 10 years earlier, replaced the agrarian socio-economic status quo with a more egalitarian arrangement where anyone could cultivate, provided that they paid a fixed sum to the East India Company for the privilege of doing so. The Palegars and other higher-status people, who preferred the old agrarian system 'represented against the decadent social order', were in many cases 'upstarts' and "were also the heirs of a social system in which various orders of Hindu society were integrated through ages". These people were dispossessed of their lands, which were then redistributed but the primary purpose of the change was to increase production rather than to restructure the social order. In some cases, it coincided with a punishment because among the dispossessed were those who had recently been involved in fighting the East India Company in the Palegar wars. Some received pensions in lieu of the lost lands but at inconsistent rates.

The changes, which included the introduction of the *ryotwari* system and other attempts to maximise revenue, deprived the village headmen and other higher-status people of their role as revenue collectors and position as landholders, while also impacting the lower-status cultivators by depleting their crops and leaving them impoverished. The population held the view that the British were taking their wealth and that those who were dependent on the traditional system no longer had the means to make a living. As the old order collapsed into disarray, the once-authoritative Palegars, including Naraşimha Reddy, became the focus of attention of the sufferers, whose pleas fell on deaf British ears. The

Palegars saw a chance to mobilise the peasant opposition, both for genuine social reasons. Narasimha Reddy's own objections too was based on their outcomes. Compared to the Palegar of Nossam, the pension awarded to his family upon their dispossession was paltry and the authorities refused to increase it by redistributing some of the Nossam money when that latter family became extinct in 1821. At the same time, some of his relatives faced proposals for further reductions in their land rights, including a reform of the village policing system.

War against British Colonials

Things came to a head in 1846 when the British authorities assumed land rights previously held by various people, who had died in the villages of Goodladurty, Koilakuntla and Nossam. Encouraged by the discontent of others, Reddy became the figurehead for an uprising.

An armed group, initially comprising those dispossessed of *inam* lands around Koilakuntla, was led by Reddy's right-hand man Vadde Obanna, in July 1846. The Acting Collector for the area, Lord Cochrane, believed that Reddy had material support from fellow pensioners in Bhagyanagar and Kurnool, whose land rights had also been appropriated. The group soon attracted support from the peasantry and was reported by British authorities to have rampaged in Koilkuntla, taking back the looted treasury and evading the police before killing several officers at Mittapally. They also plundered Rudravaram before moving to an area near Almore, where they were pursued by the British military forces who then surrounded them.

A battle between Obanna's 5000-strong band and a much smaller British force then took place, with around 200 of the freedom fighters being killed and others captured before they were able to break out in the direction of Kothakota, Giddalur, where Reddy's family were living. He and the rest of the freedom fighters moved into the Nallamala Hills. The British offered incentives for information regarding the freedom fighters, who were again surrounded amidst reports that unrest was now growing in other villages of the area. In a further skirmish between the freedom fighters and the British, who had sent for reinforcements, 40-50 freedom fighters were killed and 90 were captured, including Reddy. Although there was no evidence of Obanna's capture, he most possibly was held captive along with his leader.

Warrants were issued for the arrest of nearly 1,000 freedom fighters, of which 412 were released without charge. A further 273 were bailed and 112 were convicted. Reddy, too, was convicted and was given the death penalty. On 22 February, 1847, he was executed in Koilkuntla in front of a crowd of over 2,000 people.

The British kept his head on the fort wall in public view, until 1877. The East India Company reported in their district manual of 1886 that "since 1839, nothing of political importance has occurred, unless we mention the disturbance in 1847 caused by Narasimha Reddy, a pensioned Palegar of Uyyalawada in Koilakuntla *taluka*, then part of Kadapa district. He was in receipt of a pension of Rs.11 a month. As a grandson of Jayaram Reddy, the last powerful *zamindar* of Nossam, he was sorely disappointed when the government refused to pay him any portion of the lapsed pension of that family.

Just before this time, the question of resuming Kattubadi *inams* had been brought under the consideration of the government, which made the Kattubadis discontented. Narasimha Reddy collected these men and attacked the Koilakuntla treasury. He moved from place to place and sheltered himself in Thepi hill forts of the Erramalas and Nallamalas, and though pursued by troops from Kadapa and Kurnool, he continued to commit his ravages in Koilakuntla and Cumbum. At Giddalur, he gave battle to Lieutenant Watson and killed the *tahsildar* of Cumbum. He then escaped into the Nallamalas and after roving about the hills for several months, was caught near Perusomala on a hill in Koilakuntla *taluka* and hanged. His head remained hung on the gibbet in the fort until 1877, when the scaffold finally fell into decay."

□

73

Veerapandiya Kattabomman

(January, 1760 – 16 October, 1799)

Veerapandiya Kattabomman was an 18th-century Tamil *palayakarrar* and king of Panchalankuruchi in Tamil Nadu. He refused to accept the sovereignty of the British East India Company and waged a war against them. He was captured by the British with the help of the ruler of the kingdom of Pudukottai, Vijaya Raghunatha Tondaiman, and at the age of 39, he was hanged at Kayathar on 16 October, 1799. The historian,

Susan Bayly says that Kattabomman is considered a Robin Hood-like figure in local folklore and is the subject of several traditional narrative ballads in the *kummi* verse form. The site of his execution at Kayathar has become a 'powerful local shrine' and at one time sheep were sacrificed there. The government of Tamil Nadu maintains a memorial at Kayathar and the remnants of the old fort at Panchalankurichi are protected by the Archaeological Survey of India. In 2006, the Tirunelveli district administration organised a festival at

Panchalankurichi on his birth anniversary.

The Tamil-language film 'Veerapandiya Kattabomman', starring Sivaji Ganesan, is based on his life.

To commemorate the bicentenary of Kattabomman's hanging, the Government of India released a postal stamp in his honour on 16 October, 1999. The Indian Navy Communications Centre at Vijayanarayanam is named 'INS Kattabomman'.

□

74
Velu Nachyar

(3 January, 1730 – 25 December, 1796)

Velu Nachyar was a queen of Sivaganga estate from c. 1780-1790. She was the first Indian queen to wage war with the East India Company in India. She is known by Tamils as Veeramangai ('brave woman').

Velu Nachiyar was the princess of Ramanathapuram and the only child of King Chellamuthu Vijayaragunatha Sethupathy and Queen Sakandhimuthathal of the Ramnad kingdom.

Nachiyar was trained in many methods of combat, including war match weapons usage, martial arts like Valari, Silambam, horse riding, and archery. She was a scholar in many languages and was proficient in languages like French, English and Urdu. She married the King of Sivagangai, with whom she had a daughter. When her husband Muthu Vaduganatha Periyavudaya Thevar was killed in a battle with EIC soldiers, she was drawn into the conflict. She escaped the battlefield with her daughter.

During this period, she formed an army and sought

an alliance with Hyder Ali with the aim of launching a campaign against the East India Company, in 1780. When Velu Nachiyar found the place where the EIC stored some of their ammunition, she arranged a suicide attack on the location, blowing it up. Nachiyar re-inherited the kingdom of her husband and ruled it for ten more years. In 1790, the throne was inherited by her daughter Vellacci. She granted powers to her daughter with the Marudu brothers to help in the administration of the kingdom in 1780. Velu Nachiyar died a few years later, on 25 December, 1796.

□

75

Vinayak Damodar Savarkar

(28 May, 1883 – 26 February, 1966)

Vinayak Damodar Savarkar, commonly known as Swatantryaveer Savarkar or simply Veer Savarkar in Marathi language, was a freedom fighter and an Indian Independence activist and politician, who formulated the Hindu nationalist philosophy of Hindutva. He was a leading personality in the Hindu Mahasabha. Savarkar joined the Hindu Mahasabha and popularised the term 'Hindutva' (Hinduness), previously coined by Chandranath Basu, to create a collective 'Hindu' identity as an essence of Bharat (India). Savarkar was an atheist and also a pragmatic practitioner of Hindu philosophy.

Savarkar began his political activities as a high school student and continued to do so at Fergusson College in Pune. He and his brother founded a secret society called Abhinav Bharat Society. When he went to the United Kingdom for his law studies, he involved himself with organisations, such as India House and the

Free India Society. He also published books advocating complete Indian Independence by revolutionary means. One of the books he published, called *The Indian War of Independence*, about the Indian rebellion of 1857, was banned by the British authorities. In 1910, Savarkar was arrested and ordered to be extradited to India for his connections with the revolutionary group at India House.

On the voyage back to India, Savarkar staged an attempt to escape and seek asylum in France while the ship was docked in the port of Marseilles. The French port officials however handed him back to the British in contravention of international law. On return to India, Savarkar was sentenced to two life terms of imprisonment totalling fifty years and was moved to the Cellular Jail in the Andaman and Nicobar Islands.

After 1937, he started travelling widely, becoming a forceful orator and writer, advocating Hindu political and social unity. Serving as the president of the Hindu Mahasabha political party, Savarkar endorsed the idea of India as a Hindu *rashtra* (Hindu nation). He started his militarisation of Hindus from then on, in order to liberate the country and protect the country and Hindus in the future. Savarkar was critical of the decision taken by the Congress Working Committee in its Wardha session of 1942, passing a resolution which said to the British: 'Quit India but keep your armies here' which was the reinstallation of British military rule over India, which he felt would be much worse. In July 1942, as he felt extremely stressed carrying out his duties as the president of Hindu Mahasabha, and as he needed some rest, he resigned from the post of the president of the Hindu Mahasabha, the timing of which coincided with Gandhi's Quit India movement. In 1948, Savarkar was charged as a co-conspirator in the assassination of Mahatma Gandhi; however, he was acquitted by the court for lack of evidence. Savarkar resurfaced in the popular discourse after the coming of the Bharatiya Janata Party (BJP) into power in 1998 and again in 2014, with the Modi-led BJP government at the Centre.

On 8 November, 1963, Savarkar's wife, Yamuna, died. On 1 February, 1966, Savarkar renounced medicines, food and water and this he termed as *atmaarpan* (fast until death). Before his death, he had written an article titled '*Atmahatya Nahi Atmaarpan*', in which he argued that when one's life mission is over and the ability to serve society is left no more, it is better to end the life at will rather than waiting for death. His condition was described to have become as 'extremely serious' before his death on 26 February, 1966, at his residence in Bombay (now Mumbai). He faced difficulty in breathing; efforts to revive him failed and he was declared dead at 11:10 a.m. (IST) that day. Prior to his death, Savarkar had asked his relatives to perform only his funeral and do away with the rituals of the 10th and 13th day of the Hindu faith. Accordingly, his last rites were performed at an electric crematorium in Bombay's Sonapur locality by his son Vishwas, the following day.

He was mourned by large crowds that attended his cremation. He left behind a son Vishwas and a daughter Prabha Chiplunkar. His first son, Prabhakar, had died in infancy. His home, possessions and other personal relics have been preserved for public display. There was no official mourning by the then Congress government of Maharashtra or at the Centre. The political indifference to Savarkar continued long after his death. □

Aao Saath Chalen

'Aao Saath Chalen' is an organisation engaged in social work for the last nine years, under the leadership of Dr. Vishnu Mittal. The campaign was initiated for environmental protection and promotion. Today new dimensions are being established in the socio-cultural, economic, educational and environmental fields. It will not be an exaggeration to say that the successful experiments of Panch 'J' promotion can be directly seen and admired. Its description is as follows.

It is said that 'Pahla Sukh Nirogi Kaya' is necessary; for this, nutritious food and timely treatment of the needy is essential. Patients from all over the country come to RML hospital for treatment, but due to lack of proper information, they used to keep asking here and there for treatment and other daily needs. Today selflessly, the volunteers of 'Aao Saath Chalen' help the patients day and night, providing stretchers immediately or escorting them to the doctor on a wheel chair. How and which doctor's prescription should be made for OPD, all these works are done by these selfless persons with great intimacy.

The attendants of the patients also go through agony and mental stress. They keep on running have and there hungry and thirsty. Neither it is possible to leave the patient alone in the hospital and go any where to eat food; also it is not possible to eat nutritious food due to financial constraints. The organisation found a solution for this by establishing 'Prasadam'. Every day thousands of patients are served nutritious food to the attendants of the patients. Presently Ram Manohar Lohia Hospital and Safdarjung Hospital in Delhi and Government Hospital in Kotputli, Rajasthan serve different meals on all seven days of the week from Prasadam Rath, so that proper and nutritious diet can be provided to the attendants of the patients. Mittalji and his team found a unique solution to ensure that the activity of 'Prasadam' continues and does not become a financial burden on anyone. Team members celebrate their own and their acquaintances' birthdays, wedding anniversary or any other special day by sponsoring meals through Prasadam. And everyday new members are joining this celebration, eventually contributing to the meals of the needy.

In Delhi's severe winter, several homeless and poor people are seen shivering and braving the chilly winds. These deprived people do not have winter cloting or blanket to save themselves from the cold wave. Showing humanity, the 'Aao Saath Chalen' team established a free blanket bank at RML Hospital three years ago. Today, in addition to this blankets are being distributed at various places in Delhi and Kotputli.

One can see a glimpse of harmony with nature in the 'Vastram' campaign. Through this, the team is trying to collect new and old clothes, books and toys. Cooperation in this campaign will not only bring a smile on the face of needy and poor but also promote environmental protection by not delimbing, the and thriving old clothes here and there. For this a showroom has been made in

Kotputli where old clothes are washed and ironed. To ensure that the clothes fit well to the person who comes to pick these old clothes, tailor has also been appointed there.

In Indian thought, a specific vision in the context of nature or the expression of its relationship with nature is *Panch Mahabhoota, Panch Tattvarahi*. Thinking about them in his work and religion, Dr. Vishnu Mittal has been doing everything for their balance with a natural feeling. This thinking was carried out by the organisation that revived the old traditions by establishing an emotional connection of the people with water-forest-land-creatures. Today ten ponds, wells, stepwells have been revived in the villages of Kotputli. The reservoirs which had been piles of garbage for years are now quenching the thirst of the people there. Along with this, the ground water level and has also increased.

Villages which had their own Gochars, *Orans*, were rugged and their ignored or became victims of encroachment for a few decades. The organisation did the work of bringing all of them back into the fold of the society; tree plantation was done in the hilly areas, they were groomed. A garderner was appointed. In order that the people of Bagaon could get good quality fruits in their homes, selected fruit plants of best variety from all over the country were distributed. Today, lemon, malta, guava, ber, papaya, cilantro, pomegranate, khejdi trees can be seen flourishing in every house.

If we have our own village, our own farm, then the village should also have its own small cowshed. Only a decentralised system can be effective for the care of cows, its hallmark is in Sudarpura village. A tin shed has been built to protect the cows from the sun, cold and rain, and a store was built for fodder collection. It is a home for generously dontate 50-55 cows, for whom the villagers and friends for fodder, water, grains and other arrangements.

Be it the lakhs of birds flying around the Nada temple or the hundreds of monkeys living in the ravines of Shahpura Tirahe, the organisation makes arrangements for drinking water for them over the years. The birds are fed two quintals of barley, jowar, bajra, wheat, gram and maize in the form of pellets, while the monkeys are fed seasonal fruits or one and a half quintals of wheat flour every day.

To ensure that no one is deprived of education due to financial constraints, the team has been doing all possible help for smooth education for any a request for help from any corner of the country.

If someone is not getting good treatment due to poor financial conditions, or if the donation of a poor girl has stopped, then she is also helped by the organisation. Financial assistance is being given every month to the families of the victims of the horrific fire incident in Mundka, Delhi.

Self-employment training centre was established in Dhadha village to make rural women self-reliant. Self-reliance will increase the self-confidence of rural women. Under this training, women are making cloth bags, mats, decorative items, earthen lamps, pendants for Diwali decorative lights, bouquets, clip boards, bedsheets etc.

□□□